Blacker Than Shakespeare's INK:

The Diary Of A Nostalgic Kid

By: Cordney "MAC Woods" McClain

First Print - 2018

ISBN-13: 978-1546474357
ISBN-10: 1546474358

◆MAC WOODS◆

Cover Production: Crystell Publications
We Help You Self-Publish Your Book
(405) 414-3991

Printed in the USA

BLACKER THAN SHAKESPEARE'S INK:
THE DIARY OF A NOSTALGIC KID

DEDICATION

I dedicate this to the reader. The person I have not met yet, the one I will never meet, and my loved ones that may have purchased this book but will never read it. The person that doubted that this book would be a reality, the person who wanted this for me before I wanted it for myself, the person who secretly despises all of my successes, and the person who listened to and read my poems over and over because I am my biggest critic. This is for the person who heard my poetry and showed a lack of interest. This is for the person that I don't know at well but they're always rooting for me from afar.

I dedicate this to all of you because you all are about to become subject to my worst nightmare; the time in which you find out all of my deepest thoughts. Enjoy!

CONTENTS

BLACKER THAN SHAKESPEARE'S INK:
THE DIARY OF A NOSTALGIC KID

ACKNOWLEDGMENTS

I could never thank everyone that has influenced my writing or my spirit but please see the following as my best effort:

First and foremost to God. In whatever form I decide to worship; I just know someone greater than I has been protecting and moving me for an immensely long time. Thank you.

To my family. My mother, Ms. Juliette McClain, you are my first source of inspiration and the first to tell me to write a book. My wife, Mrs. Carrie McClain, your belief in me made me a better man. To my late Grandmother, Ms Velma Jean McClain and the whole McClain family, you are all my back bone and I strive for greatness to make you proud. To my big brother and uncle, Mr. Victor Guyton and Mr. Reginald McClain, more like two fathers; you both are greatly appreciated for relentless encouragement through my adolescence. Thank you.

To my daughters. Ms. Kimora and Ms. Camílla, you are so young and do not even realize to the extent that you have both inspired me to be more for you and myself. Thank you.

To my brethren. Mr. Kai Phoenix (whom assisted in the title of this book), Dr. Michael Chapman Jr, Mr. Deangelo Rodgers, Mr. Reginald Phipps, and Mr. Corey Hanes, five men who were always open to read my work and kept me inspired. To all of the "crew", most of this book is about you, well us. I took from you and it helped me evolve as a man. Thank you.

To my illustrator. Mr. Billie Allen, I requested your services and you delivered beyond my expectations. Thank you.

To my 8th grade Creative Writing teacher. Ms. Stephanie Cochran, you are the reason that I ever picked up a pen and tried to write down my thoughts. Thank you.

Last but not least, to Mrs. Crystal Carter, you brought me under your wing, gave me so many priceless gems, and accelerated my book publishing process. Thank you.

Black Cordney!

"Black Cordney! You shiny black like my shoes,
So black that you could show up naked at funerals,
So black when you go outside the street lights turn on
So black when you was born,
God said, "Damn I dun burnt another one"..
Black Cordney, my reflection was masked,
Cause it's reflective of the mass
And they want you fair skinned and smiling so bright..
I'll be honest, in the 1st grade I told my teacher I wanted to be white.
He asked me why and I replied,
"Cause their hair moved in the water...
All of them have their father, you think they're all way smarter...
And I would be able to find the perfect marker...
To draw and color myself."

And I learned early that was self-hate that had I harbored...

Until it became much clearer about the reflection in the mirror.
The fair skinned was bragging about their
Great Grandmother being raped by her slave master...
The secrets on their face of slavery being revealed
What their grandfather couldn't stop or would've been killed for
The slave master murdered his children and raped his wife.
He raped her daily and the screams were heard all the way to the fields;
Their grandmother would close her eyes to take herself away
Back, back to her homeland while the master had his pants
Down to his ankles and told her to never speak of this
And the woman of the big house held resentment.
So over and over she whipped the raped victim;
For her husband's unfaithfulness then the rape of her humanity gave
Birth to the cry of **babies that were born half white.**

And this skin is kind of light and the baby is confused but feels special
Cause the overseer of the slaughter is now bi-racial...
But three-fifths of them...still it is and the inability
Of the husband to protect his wife and kids
Has had the black man running from his family ever since.
Then the essence of what Black beauty was...
Is mutated into blonde hair, blue eyes, and a lack of melanin.
And *"you shol' is cute for a girl that's dark skin."*
Is supposed to be taken as the highest compliment.

"Ewww, you sholll' is ugly"...
And not tragically colored, not an ounce or an inch.
There is no great sorrow damned up in my soul,
Nor lurking behind my eyes. I do not mind at all.
Dark as the midnight hour, but souls' bright as the mornin' Sun...
All of my traits didn't make me a victim;
I learned that all that hated my dazzling dye was fearsome
Including some Black folks, simply prejudice against our own race.
We gone learn eventually to stop playin' these ol' paper bag games.

Inspired by Saul Williams "Black Stacey" (2004)

3

A Fiend of the High
Orientation:

I was high way before the needle stopped...
Hello...my name is Cordney...and I'm an addict.
My first time, Marvin Gaye was on Mom's record player.
My memory escapes but it rhymed some words like...
"Crack heads...my niggas dead...and got my ass whooped by the cops".
I spit if for my uncle and it was really about his life.
The dope boy sat back with an expression somewhat ghost like.
"Boy, how you see so much at age 9?"
And that's the first time I learned how to write.
Escaping from this excavation, my words evolved into rhymes;
Black people tied to trees, I took a deep dive...
Into their wounds bubbled up from their spines.
Political prisoners spoke to me that predicted our history.
Bombs to black churches, the smoke was choking my lungs
Seeing papa and mama getting hung...
Revolution so young in tears carrying a ton.
Subconsciously, why niggas get blazed maybe?
Tryin' to find their way to the sun.

A Fiend of the High

Power Struggle:

This oh so beautiful medicine...most beautiful medic I ever seen
To fill this emptiness inside of me..."*IT KEEP CALLLIN' ME!*"
When depression sets in, it's the prescription I take.
Dries my mouth, eyes both blood shot,
Fighting family cause they could finally read my thoughts.
The man in the mirror is my addict and he will do whatever for this shit
Pushing tons of this dopeness through my veins.
My mind's demons SCREAMING ALL OVER A PAGE.
Shit, I'm HIGH RIGHT NOW!.. Excuse me while I do another line....
The cravings even control my day, engrosses my mind-my time,
Taking me away from my family...
See, I hurry my daughters to sleep just so I can write about their dreams.
DAMN, YOU DON'T KNOW WHAT THIS DRUG DOES TO ME!

A Fiend of the High
Synergy:

This shit right here, my nigga, THIS SHIT RIGHT HERE!
Will exploit your desires and let loose your fears.
Columns so raw, you'll line em' up on a mirror...
Just to watch the dope take over your mind.
The temptations stronger than mistresses
In short dresses sitting in the front pew.
Holding myself in dark corners of my mind, plottin'...
Of some rhymes more iller than a threatening ailment.
I'm on more than some bomb threat in the mail shit.
My cerebellum is a mix of Damien, Shining, and Kruger.
See, a child surrounded by satanic forces who dreams of a horrific future.
That grew into a writer with visions of the past,
Haunting a well-spoken, skin broken Logan.
No longing for bandages, has an edification to heal quick.
Yes, being a mutant has its advantages.
Cursing in cursive, painful memories that hurt to say.
I've become addicted to clever word play.
Nouns that rip the sky, vicious verbs, and double entendres.
Provocative narratives knotted with mysterious adjectives.
Every morning I open my eyes to assess the damages.
I'm just so poetic who's becoming use to usin' his narcotic.
SHIT! Here I go relapsing over again!

A Fiend of the High

Closure:

I'm REHABILITATING but still feelin' REBELLIOUS!
Close my eyes, tap the page, and just let a lil hell in.
Pull out my syringe, playing in my mind when I zone;
WOOO! tell me "What's Going On"...so timeless.
And then I vent, for all my lost feelings, a moment of silence....
Reason why I write then go get the copyright.
So the vulnerability of my emotions that I deny...
Will at least forever BE ALL MINE.

Hello...my name is Cordney...and I'm just a fiend of the high.

Inspired by Prentice Powell "Addiction" (2015)

Black Jesus

The classroom was silent with shocking anger and amazement of my proclamation and the teacher in disbelief, both seemed so heartbroken. *"JESUS WAS BLACK!"* I delivered a message so disturbing that it would roast their Easter Rabbit, hang their Santa Clause, and rape their Tooth Fairy beliefs. Within the walls of this Christian private school, in the red state-Bible Belt of Oklahoma, that held services every other day and had scripture in their actual learning plan and syllabus, a little black boy had just deemed the man that died on the cross for these little white children was indeed a Black man. We were in the midst of the eminent "Easter Resurrection" story with pictures to portray and I stood up and shattered their dreams.

If Jesus is real, and was born in Bethlehem, a descendant of Israel then given the location on the continent of Africa, combined with hints in the Book of Solomon depicting his grandmother then he had to be a black man and the Bible never portrays any signs of his appearance as being a marker for him to be cast out or discriminated against. The history of human nature shows that if he looked different than the rest of his peers, it would have been noted and tremendously recognized. A pale white man similar to an Ashton Kutcher or Christian Bale in a sea of Black folks would have made some type of commotion. "He had hair of wool and complexion was the color of burnt brass...THAT LOOKS LIKE ME, not the picture hanging up in every black church that I've been in!" A moment of silence and then a blare of "NO, NO, NO!" from the sea of white children that filled my classroom began to roar.

The teacher, with nothing to rebuttal, escorted me out and to the principal's office. They called my Momma but I couldn't decipher if I was in trouble or not. They stated that I upset the other students and had to be removed from class.

Years later, at the University of Oklahoma in my sophomore public speaking course, I presented a persuasive speech entitled "The Black Man Named Jesus" among yet again a classroom of all white peers. Surprisingly though in this instance, most of them agreed with the evidence I presented and gave me a great amount of respect for the presentation and research. In that kindergarten class, I received my first lesson: the real world is a white world and it does not desire to hear what you have to say when your beliefs conflict with their value system or puts a mirror up to their indignity. In any case, always hold on to what your heart believes, do the research no matter how taboo the stance, and at the end of the day when you speak, KNOW YOUR SHIT!

It Was Written

I SWEAR I'M A GOOD MAN...I just like sinning...
I grew up in a church front pew;
Baptized young cause Momma wanted me to.
Skinny shivering body in that cold pool.
Suppose to keep me outta hell and send me to our father.
Eluded to a daddy that I never knew so I felt familiar with the illusion.
Missing the meaning, devouring communion.
"Man, I shol was hungry, may I get another juice and cracker."
Staring at Ms. Jenkins...always catching the Holy Ghost.
My Momma pinched me for my laughter.
I grew up confused to question or free my ambiguity;
Talked to the moon and stars, they spoke silence so fluently.
In a cold world where everyone and their momma got a motive;
Atheist blame slavery and the need to feel devoted.
But when I bench press tribulations; that sensation's insulting.
Got some temptation or corruption, Brotha which one you indulging?
Regardless of what you pick, know this world's makeup is pain
And your foundation, whatever it is, better be focused.
Because death for all of us is just right around the corner.

Truthfully, I'm having a hard time being a good Christian.
Searching for answers, guess it was a kid's nature;
Felt like somebody held me when I felt doom...
Maybe that's what my pastor meant by "the spirits in the room".

The warmth of the church house, I couldn't refuse.
But all pastors, I couldn't trust cause even the devil was an angel once.
We can't believe what we can't see, reality seems stronger than prayer.
Still cursing his name when my family funerals kept coming.
Still hurt over Grandma then my aunt gets shot in the stomach.
Stinging my eyes and I was just cutting the first layer of the onion.
Uncle passed, no insurance so family fighting over funeral funding.
I heard knowledge through his word is the find...
And none of us are Stevies, you know,
Seeing the most beautiful designs while blind.
I'm so close to Heaven, Hell, I JUST NEED SOME TIME.
So yes, God got me like Mel, believing in "Signs" and at the same time...
Pastor asked for offering but...PAIN IS ALL I CAN OFFER HIM.

Tears running down my face and the choir's angels singing...
In front of me, sentiment is deep but how you gone tell the truth...
To a crowd of those that won't believe.
Bared witness within my wilderness, he filled my water pots with wine.
Lost in bitterness, fought off my villainous,
He brought light to my dark nights.
Till I leave with what most sold, my soul.
I'm just a rose in some weeds, indeed.
Pressing hard, Stay-Flo till I leave my crease;
With a faith like a garden and to my nonbelievers...
I say, "*I SIMPLY BELIEVE*" cause...
When I was alone, I know I felt an unexplainable comfort take over me.
And I can't say it was "God" or "Jesus" but it was much bigger than me.

And he said, "*My son all you need is a seed...all you need is a seed.*"

Lost in the World

WHY EVERYTHANG THAT'S BAD FOR ME FEEL SO GOOD?

I'm lost in the World; she's taking over my mind.
Heaven in my eyes but love making me blind.
Blind of the worldly things I'm leaving behind.
Escaping from between Earth's spread thighs...
Remind me of my heart swelling, the bulge of Mary's belly.
For a greater cause prevailing but expectance got the Emperor hailing.
And that's raining down, my own screams sound is ultra now.
Flood currents for liquid lost, an inkling of light while I crown.
Herod's prenatal genocide, moon and stars deep in eternity's eye.
Mother North Star shall she be my guide.
Nurturing how the Devil and I preside.
Immaculate Conception for how I arrived.
I'm made from the dust of the ground then born a lover
Became so got damn infatuated of her.

WHY EVERYTHANG THAT'S BAD FOR ME FEEL SO GOOD?
My deviant pouring liquor down my throat,
Blowing weed through my lungs.
Sugar coated nostrils tickling the lover's speed under my tongue.
Fighting her power, paralyzed to things that I shouldn't.
If pain is pleasure, I'm orgasmic from her charm;
Too comfortable in the sin I'm in, holding me in her arms.
A menstrual lady and I'm no Swayze, she's neither Goldberg...

So it's not my ability to control her.
She's time unraveling, seconds gone by, that's been weeks.
GIVE ME MY SOUL BACK, DEVILISH WORLD!
I wish the love exchange came with a couple of receipts.
So I captured her after delight in the midst of her night.
And pressed over her face a pillow of release,
Kicking with violent rage, my grip grew with strength and...
Her antagonizing left scratches to my face.
I could hear her breathes getting shorter.
Body became limp and her influence grew weak.
I held her lifeless being closer to me.
As my soul lost from this hoarder and her pain flooding the sheets.
Then the heavens rumbled... I COULD SEE THE LIGHT!
My body elevated...I was floating among the heavens.
I can see my departed World at my feet.
And her beautiful ugly hands still pulling for me.

LOST IN THE WORLD.

WAVES
Waded Adaptation Vindicating Exceeding Success

"I USE TO HAVE THE WAVES, MAN!...

Summer '96, or was it '95, or was it spring time, hell, never mind....
I was on the corner with my uncle boomin' Too Short while I'm acting
Like I ain't dissecting the words while drawing Ninja Turtles.
Mike Tyson Punch Out, Penny Hardaway's with the tongue out.
Hide and Go Get It, Kool Aid pickles, Chico Stickin',
Picking my own switches; young thundercats catching fire flies.
Nigga Knockin', paper footballs, Dip n Stix was all live.
Big Chew, Ring Pops..."MAN, *DON'T TOUCH MY LEMON DROPS!*"
Then to 99', I'm trynna hook my waves up, trynna keep my grades up.
Damn, the girls lookin' so grown with mo' ass and mo' makeup.
To 01', I'm smelling like Burger King French fries...
Sneaking chicks outta my room before my mama wake up.
Before I ever knew love and the hurt of a breakup.
Before niggas kicked my mama's door in for the shakeup.
Record and play on my boom box to catch Tupac on cassette tapes...
But sneaking Mozart in my headphones.
Right before my goatee start forming...
Right after I started feeling awkward in who I was becoming.

"I used to put a hot towel on my head after I brushed for a while...
My whole head damn near white from the thick ass grease.
My shit was spinning b, SPINNING!"

Peer pressure had vice grips on me...so...
Me and my niggas, three deep in a black Cutlass Supreme.
Almost on 'e'", bumping "Get Rich" to "Street Dreams".
Mom's glocc laying on my Polo jeans next to some Mickey D's;
Large sweet tea, small fry, two McChickens with cheese.
On a mission for a nigga, use to be the homie, now a dope fiend.

From Oakcliff to Hartsdale, Soutside, 3105;
Police took one look and claimed gang relations was our lives.
So yea I grew up with killas but I ain't know they was killas.
And I knew how to cook crack...
Before Short Dogg gave Caine the work in the kitchen.
Thought it was cool till Unk was sent away for the work in his kitchen.
The only father figure I ever knew, hoping he'd notice my waves...
As I avoided eye contact in the visiting room.

"LIL NIGGA, YOU GOT HEART, RIGHT, YOU GOT HEART?"
Lumpin' and slap boxing, seeing who's harder in the school yard.
Free styling in home room, politicin' for free lunch.
Sitting low in Language Arts, avoiding desires to be too smart.
Corner store jacking Trojans to never impregnate somebody's daughter.
Tried to wrap it up twice so scared of being a father.
Snuck on the roof like Queen, Jada, and Vivica with asthmatic lungs...
Puff, puff, and passed anyway, an only child so did it all for the love.
Then introduced too early to being a man attending too many wakes.
I had just told Nino to slow down before he met his fate.
And I just dapped up Twank before he caught that case.
Didn't wanna be another black boy stuck regretting mistakes.
But I couldn't tell the homies none of that...
I just heard the news, sat back into myself, and brushed down my fade.

"I USE TO HAVE THE WAVES, MAN!
Murrays - Pink Luster was my thang; Du Rag on all damn day,
Man, I remember way back when."

16

18 at Will

LAST WILL AND TESTAMENT OF...."Endangered Black Boy".
I, Endangered Black Boy, not yet a man residing at every corner of the world, being of no sound mind, declare this to be my Last Will and Testament. I revoke because I never knew, pardon previous, they kept hidden the wills previous of my own. The world in my words, my putrid esophagus. I thirst for a father but he called in absent. Well he was around but didn't see him on some Ghost Dad shit. So I was a legitimate bastard.

ARTICLE I
An experiment of my environment. Born just to die. Before driver's licenses, we cruise in hearses so I appoint the Streets as my Personal Representative to administer this Will. If the Streets are unwilling or unable to serve, then I appoint my Seed that I reproduced to be another victim.

ARTICLE II
I direct my Personal Representative (The Streets) to pay out of my residuary estate all of the expenses of my last illness, which was all of the hurt that I bottled up. From my momma I never knew, who did drugs, to selling crack rock to people who look like me, to my play uncle that put my head in his lap and rubbed my behind in his Cadillac among dark alleys; this for the latest Jordans and food to eat because Big Momma never had much. I never could trust another man with that type of

growing up and my manhood was always a skeptical crutch.

With all taxes and what the Governmental charges impose, I have nothing but a big open heart and this smaller casket closed. Closed from the defamation that I suffered even before I was potty trained the police profiled me and teachers could see a criminal in my tender 3rd grade seat. My high school counselors said I wouldn't see the age of 20. I had to rush to write this document before I reached 18. For the purpose that this is all the life expectancy that the world has given me.

ARTICLE III

I devise, bequeath, and give my distrust for any brother that looks just like me. I devise, bequeath, and give my absence to my son to inherit my ways to continue the absentee family customs. I devise, bequeath, and give my disappointment to Big Momma that always prayed over me.

ARTICLE IV

Should any beneficiary not survive me by 30 days, his or her share shall be distributed to his or her then surviving children in equal shares for the continuance of my despair.

ARTICLE V

The Personal Representative and Executor of this Will shall receive no compensation for his or her services. The Guardian appointed hereunder shall receive no compensation for his services hereunder because they were never there.

ATTESTATION

Endangered Black Boy (TESTATOR)

WITNESSES: Gang Violence
Public Housing
Corrupt Government System
Out of Touch Politicians
Generational Poverty

PTSD

POST TRAUMATIC SLAVE DISEASE!

I got a letter from the Gov'ment the other day...
I opened and read it, it said, "NIGGER, YOU STILL A SLAVE!"
Been proven by the system that the ink of politicians...
Are worth more than the blood of us victims.
We became colonists and dropped consciousness,
Population control from food to mentality to us killing us.
Gangs, prison, and drugs, all growing up looking for some form of love.
Heart ends up cold so with the heat we fall in love...
Amerikkka the beautiful, oh the home of the brave,
Picking cotton overseas for Tricare and student aid.
An old black man that worked all his life...
On his hand and knees told me,
"Be careful son, that shit'll send you to your grave."
Heavy burdens since the doctor slapped my ass
Mightest well been my face.
"*Nigga here...hold that and that and some mo' of that.*"
That's assistance truancy, oppressive influences, stereotyping nuances,
And you better be at drill, they have way more brainwashing...
To do before you kill at will.... Keep it in step, now!

Stay in line, boy, adopt this slave state of mind, boy.
A pessimist screaming "*FUCK THE POLICE!*"..
Absurdly stated in my Army green.
A psychological dictatorship, over confederate patriotic fools,
Overzealous to deploy, overdoing form of Herod's rule.
Killing baby boys, in fear his kingdom will be destroyed
The food is contaminated, the water is too,
Babies require vaccination for the flu...
That then gives them the flu and keeps them from school.
That's war against consciousness honoring racists
Who been your president so...
Trumped ignorance been well accepted and the Gov'ment kept it.
In step, keep it in step, now!

20

We dry mouthed, parched for the constitution?
Shit, I want retribution and I wear the uniform,
A sign of my prostitution.
POST TRAUMATIC SLAVE DISEASE!
Oooh Lady Liberty...that bitch lied to me, put hands on me
And claimed, "Baby, I'll never do it again."
I clung to her, made excuses for her, loved her; too much to walk away.
My reflection of affection became coping with the pain.
Abuse and remind me daily that nobody else could love me anyway,
Oh, Lady Liberty...
With our own testicles shoved in our complacent mouths
Batteries in our backs,
Molotovs in our eyes so I rep the colors that fed the animals;
GET THE HOUNDS!...
That hunted Huey P. and Malcolm X down!
POST TRAUMATIC SLAVE DISEASE!

I will always place the mission first, I will never accept defeat.
I will never quit, I will never leave a fallen comrade.
But where was America the 500 years when they left me?...
I am a soldier, convinced it's all for a worthy cause.
I am a soldier, no genuine thought since I signed on that dotted line.
I am a soldier, missing a leg and arm but praised for a medical discharge.
I am a solider, so honored I'm homeless from being so mentally scarred.
I am a soldier, so I shut my damn mouth, take orders....and die;

And when that folded flag gets so carefully creased, so precise...
Then handed to my momma, while the pain crushes her.
She accepts sacrificing her only child...
For serving her country that never served her...
Don't tell me what I'm fighting for on battlefields that we never leave.
Don't thank me for my service now but you want me to forget slavery.

Don't tell me to adapt and overcome...
I'VE ADAPTED AND OVERCAME SINCE I WAS BORN!
Right here in America, suited up with armor but...
My melanin can't make me feel safe yet.

"You're grieving? HELL NEVER MIND, PARADE REST, BOY!...
Matta fact, coon, SALUTE IN THESE SINISTER TIMES!"

Then BOOOOM!...The brother exploded, the system pulled the trigger.
One more young bouquet of roses, the brother became a nigger.
And they ask, "Wow, Sweet Jesus, how did this happen?"...
They set up the chair, wrote the letter, and we helped tie up the noose.
Well...they're accustomed to killin' black men...and we are too.
So now I live in this mind, sit in the head of this shit that they design.
Selling hope with despair, a world consumed with an eye for an eye.
And they're still blind...so we're all blind.
THEY'RE STILL BLIND SO WE'RE ALL BLIND.

POST TRAUMATIC SLAVE DISEASE!

Heaven's Afternoon
(Ms. Velma Jean)
Jan 17 1935 – Mar 31 1999

I remember Momma told me *"Grandma went to a better place"*.
I didn't wanna hear it, played dumb, deaf to it, and slow....
I just know you wasn't here to hold me no mo'.
Rhyming on wet paper just to let my tears out.
I'd pay the rent to stay in the Lord's house.
If Heaven was a mile away, I'd hold and kiss your face
Tell you how much I love you, all the things...
I ain't know how to say at age 14; I use to make you coffee.
In that small black pot on the front left eye
While you sat in your corner chair watching your stories
I never knew being without you would still haunt me...

Looking to Heaven...now I close the windows to my soul
To revisit the beauty of your eyes...
And even at the age of 5, looking out your window to the moon
The fireflies dancing with the street light
You spoke with me on the beautiful struggle of life
God showed me in a dream that an angel would absolutely love me....
I awoke from 17 years of slumber and can still feel you hold me
The greatest gift you ever gave me...
But the years go by and it's hard for me to hear your voice
It's getting harder for me to feel your kiss
It's getting harder for me remember your hugs
I have a piece of you still here in my mother
But she makes it so hard to be loved cause we never see eye to eye...
Family gatherings aren't the same and...
We hold on too tight to every grudge
I just wish you were here to show us how to love.
To tell me "I will see you soon but to appreciate this time".
To comfort your daughter's son
Hold me, call me your lil Huckleberry, and remind...
"Baby, baby, everything's going to be just fine".
So never good bye but Happy Birthday...
I will see you up in the sky or every night when I close my eyes.

My Brother's Keeper

"AM I MY BROTHER'S KEEPER? Yes, yes, I am!"...Although, I'm worried he will break my heart. As he walks into my home with the smile that lights up the room, a smile I remember that got him out of shit so many times again and again as a 9 year old boy and now as a grown 30 year old man. It now weighs heavy on my heart that he could bypass our life long relationship for a little bit of money for a moment of substance. And how stubborn I have become, I know I would push him away forever if he hurt me to an extent of my own personal "no return". I'm afraid of losing our relationship; the lacking there of that still resides. My family always told me coming up that when I was a baby, I rarely even spoke until he was born. He was as big as me and I would try to pack him around and called him "my baby".

From ass whoopings, fist fights, girl's booties, Nintendo, Starter Jackets, and basketball, I was aspired to be there for him or whoop anybody's ass that may have tried to bring friction to my "lil bro". And "lil bro" is what he has always been to me. Nothing like a cousin, son of my aunt with a different father that lived two hours away that I saw on holidays, and may spend a portion of the summer with. We caught fireflies, picked out Grandma's switches together, stayed up all night talking about life at those tender ages but with an old man's understanding. Life taught us different lessons; lessons that drove him away from his mother but made me respect mine even more. The outcomes from criminal activity that pushed me to excel in education had seemed to lure him with a whore's temptation. Outcomes that our eyes shared that resulted in him wanting to run away from family but brought me closer to ours. Though in the midst of these developing breaches among our personal moral compasses, we were growing up as brothers in the same household, sharing each other's clothes, sleeping in the same bed; him at the head and me at the foot.

I have always hoped he saw me as the big brother that he never had. I wanted to be someone he could look up to but over the years I could tell he was running away from any similarities that could be placed between him and I. That was the first harsh reality I had to face about our relationship and that came as young as age 8 for me. The second would come in our early 20s when he began becoming a person that was unrecognizable to me. Someone that didn't want to be around family, harmed close ones for his own gain, and seemed to not be bothered by cheating anyone in his way. This is the time I began feeling like if given the opportunity, he would do the same to me, this stranger in front of me with this "oh so familiar" bright smile that I can remember as a young boy. And if that took place then I know I would want to metaphorically shoot G-Money on the rooftop in the midst of my escape and remove him from my life forever. I would give him anything from my last Snack Pack to $50 to hold him over until his check comes in. This brings me to the concept of "Survivor's Guilt".

Maybe this is guilt that I feel. I survived trauma, though him a bit more, but I have become a form of success; a contributing member of society if you will. He seems to be fighting that station of evolution. I believe my compassion for him and my motivation to do the opposite of our circumstances has compelled me to do for him still to this day. I would give him my last and he's always known that so that's why I am so afraid of my "lil bro" breaking my heart.

People Watching I

He is me and I am him...so please don't let us be misunderstood.

Man, even when I was little...
He thought being a daddy would be super cool.
I never had one so the absence gave him super fuel.
So in high school in hind sight he replaced a baby daddy.
I loved the girl so he took over gladly.
Years passed by domestic situations.
She forget, ungrateful that he is not the dog that went to flee.
And they fight with the lil boy waiting outside the ring...
Because she sees him moving on with his life and couldn't bring...
Herself to do the same...so now fatherhood became
Nothing but visitation...he tried some conversation...
Even though my momma told him never talk to fools.

Spoke to God, feeling like his child again...
I asked the Lord…on his knees crying….
"SHIT, what should he do?"...
I was having nightmares with his eyes open
When he could pick my son up from school...
To hold my boy in his arms...
Now the taste in my mouth is just his salty pool.
I know his son's momma will never tell the truth.
And damn...I never wanted my son to have an absentee father too
He turned away from the mirror and tried to comfort me.
Cause the fallacy of him being sad couldn't come from me.

And we all know that if you fake it long enough...it takes over us.
Used substitutions in disregard as a fan, I'm in the stands.
Watching him from afar...and far from moving forward
And replaced with a backcourt of guards.
Shit...I feel like our Momma never told us it would be this hard.
To the heavens, bright lights in the midst of clouds and then...
Spoke to God, feeling like his child again
Said *"Lord let him live so I can make you proud again"*.

People Watching....

The Dreamer's Sons

Flames circled our feet, one of God's gifts faced

And this is tomorrow's song but rather today...

My Mation in my soul, better spit it properly.

My Brain protected, sits in my groin awkwardly.

The pine called our bluff, I thank whatever god..

For we're unconquerable ergo WE ASKED FOR ANOTHER!

In Life's KUT, clasped arms of me and my link, searching...

For us some peace but none came for 9 weeks,

4 days, 4 hours, 39 minutes and 12, 13, 14, 15...

Faint not, fight on, hope renewed cause for so, so long...

Dense eye lids, swollen back pocket, blood coated pupils.

Stench heavy in my concrete sweater and tight jeans;

Rest was but seconds with little time to dream.

So we saw day visions of Krimson and Kream...

Then out of the night that covered us...

The great weight lifted from our shoulders

We stood unafraid with joyous tears.

ON OUR WAY DOWN TO KAPPA LANE,

Holding our scrolls so tight, they pierced our hands.

Took the male inside of me and held him for ransom.

Grim Interlude stands as my national anthem.

Well what's brotherhood?...

"BIG BROTHER SIR, the last 3 steps are the answer!"...

MADE two men into the spirit of Digg's.

Masters of our fate, captains of our soul,

Been off line a good while now, here is where the real pledging resides.

Ohhhh my K-A-Psi, oh my Phi-Nu-Pi!

I crossed over and Dr. Sloan looked me in my eyes...

"So Son, the question I have for you, "PIMP....OR....DIE!"

NUPE, NUPE, MY BROTHERS!...WE DO THISSS!

The Obama Essays:

The Oklahoman. Published: January 16, 2009

November 4, 2008 will forever be a monumental day for me. The first reason is the history that took place but the second reason may be a bit more important in my eyes. White America saw past color and distinguished the leadership qualities, class, intelligence, and Barack Obama's love for all mankind. I felt sad that only the spirits of great abolitionists and activists of the past were not present to see this day of America's awakening. Leaders such as Frederick Douglass, Marcus Garvey, Martin Luther King Jr., Malcolm X, Fannie Lou Hamer and also regular people like my grandmother Miss Velma Jean McClain. All of whom were absent among our joyful tears, warm embraces, and the aura of this elegant glory.

But the sorrow left my body and happiness filled every corner of my soul. Tears flooded my face as our next president addressed, so eloquently, his defeat of John McCain. While watching the crowd on television, I not only saw black people but all colors and ethnicities of people weeping with admiration. This triumph was not only for us but a victory for all. A change has been craved on dry mouths of billions and with this election; our tongues were flushed with a saccharine fluid of hope. This is the first of many strides for this great nation to improve on itself and become much greater. And now, when I look into my son's eyes and tell him he can be anything in the world, I can truly mean ANYTHING.

Beloved Brotha Puppet

"When you wish upon a star, makes a lot of difference who you are...
They said here is a gift for you, to bring our 40 acres and mule,
To make all our dreams come true...."

Hundreds and hundreds of years old,
An evil, all knowing carpenter at work, Mastro Geppetto.
Constructing a man from a block of pine,
Up late into the night in the belly of hell, plotting for an heir mold...
Shaped it into a being, a puppet, with a brilliance of drive.
He imprinted the feet, the pawn's heart began to beat,
Made the hair kinky, shaped the round ears, with sharpened eyes.
He fixed his strings long, effective, but tight;
Made them lengthy so followers couldn't tell he was being hung.
Perfected an intimate perspective, gave him an eloquent tongue.
Painted him not too dark but with a deceitful tint...
And we were the Blue Fairy of believers with a wish.
A rumble in the sky, wind carried the lightning and POOF!!
The wood became President...
Desired to be real but still a slave in his fight to resist
From what his master's creation still under contract to be the catalyst.
No...WE WERE NOT READY FOR A BLACK PRESIDENT.
To disguise the mission of our heart, product of a wish upon a star...

Little Wooden head go play your part, bring a little joy to every heart
Little do you know and yet it's true, that Geppetto...
Is telling him what to do.

He wanted to be a real boy but Master had his own plans.
The perfect puppet that we've never seen....
And he looked and walked just like us, a miracle we couldn't believe.
To honor him and contradict ourselves,
Persuade the fair skinned on how much he's helped.

Like the late release of criminals that were non-violent
With a sprinkle of hip hop in the white environment.
All a charade just enough to keep us excited.
We held on to every word when his donkey ears exposed,
Tail got too long, we made excuses for the decisions he made
But no change to be had, when the puppet masters are at play.

"THERE ARE NO STRINGS ON ME, NO STRINGS ON ME!"
No strings, that's what he told us and we believed
But those strings must've meant ties to us.
Leader of the Free World with his mouth taped and hands cuffed;
Mulatto Pinocchio with hands up!
We loved him but he loved Geppetto more.
When his nose grew longer from inside the whale,
The disappearance of the courageous leader we had voted for
Now urged us to support a candidate that built her career
On underlying racist comments to diminishing our pioneers.
Then counterfeit black aid with hot sauce speeches reappeared.
The strings of the power to be at work from a ceiling mirror,
Hi-Diddle-Dee-Dee, Hi-diddle-dee-dee, Hi-diddle-dee-dee,IRO
The Burden of Representation it just might be.
History is going to think it was all on his shoulders
To be everything Dr. King and Malcolm X couldn't be;
BUT A LEGACY OF A PUPPET IT JUST MIGHT BE.

"When you wish upon a star, makes a lot of difference who you are."

Strange Fruit

Oh what of a beautifully horrifying summer day...

As I spy from behind my buoyant eyes,
I smile 'cause I might fall out if I cry.
Its freedom somewhere in the sky...
I pray the ones before me finally got to fly.
Black bodies swinging in the Southern breeze;
The white of the day be surrounding me.
Lilies playing beneath my feet, summer's day teasing my nostril's nose,
I could paint the picture with my eyes closed.
Pine influences accent the heat gracefully;
Tanning the back of my neck with its warm hands.
Windows of my soul follows the ballet of butterflies and bumble bees.
Shadows high cause the sky is cloudless....
Preoccupied with mahogany and palled chasings.
Foiling dull roots with summer rainings.
I sit back and watch the world through the eye holes in my oil paintings.
In a cemetery full of flying hawks, blue jays doing somersaults.
The sky beams down with a dazzling blue...
Without Sanctuary, my people hang more it seems in the late of June.

Adam and Eve ain't never taste no fruit like these.
Do the knowledge cause ain't no snake in these trees...
Just slipknot ropes that choke away hopes
And you don't wanna shake these leaves...
Nah, you don't wanna shake these leaves.

I remember I heard them come for me amongst the quiet.
We dashed into where the wood line is thick.
They followed running mad with riot; this journey to freedom...
TASTES of torture sprinkled with a mother's tears,
LOOKS like Heaven's days shadowed by the devil's nightmares,
SMELLS like perfumed liberation fuming of hound piss,
And SOUNDS like point blank pistol blasts scoring a somber death...
THEY WERE ON THE HUNT!
Chased beyond what we knew as our reservoir;
Wildin' pursuers, we prayed with our face to the jungle floor.
Conversations with the trees while levitated souls among the stars...
Though we often forget how to read the signs...
So shotguns painted bloody murals onto the mountain sides.
A thousand pieces of heart, a third a human, an ounce of eyes.

"Pastoral scene of the gallant South.
The bulgin' eyes and the twisted mouth.
Scent of magnolias so sweet and fresh...
Then the sudden smell of burnin' flesh."

My diaspora diminished to nothing but memories on plantation crochets.
I find myself humming along with ballots of Oorun's sunrays
Or bathing in the rain to catch the sky's bouquet.
I fell asleep hanging over the flowers...
Oooh, what of a beautiful day...oooh, what of a beautiful day.

Inspired by Nina Simone "Strange Fruit" (1965)

Her Interpretation

HEY HOE! Where is the sweet little girl that I use to know?

She smokes a blunt, pops a pill, and opens her legs...
Time spent too often on her back that she couldn't afford
Long before she knew her body, her momma called her "whore".
We all don't have the strength to be a martyr
And this angel just had to live earth a little harder...

Baby Phat tanks with jean overalls, bandana too;
She swear she was T-boz plus "Waterfalls" present in her adolescence.
So precious, home "Scandalous", no Olivia, her name Candice.
That never knew family mattered;
Hot Cheetos and Kool-Aid pickles watching Family Matters.
An advent viewer of a reality she never knew of.
30 minutes of music themed hugs.
1 Mississippi..2 Mississippi...counting slow out past the streetlights.
She never wanted to go home; playing "hide n go get it"...
Never could get it, childhood games in search of fairytale happy endings.
The cause of her misery I always wondered...
So to see a smile on her face I'd buy her favorite diamond ring suckers.
A mind drunk mumbling over a sober tongue...
Was her mother, so harsh to her daughter so young.
Who had the saddest eyes of loneliness just looking to be loved....

She would stare at me and never blink;
Like we got caught in the web of each other's souls and began to sink.
About age 7, she started writing me letters...
Then I tried to keep her closer than ever...

"Hey C, me and momma went to therapy today...
I got to pick a drawing book and a toy for me to play with;
In an old room, that stinks, with ugly mustard wall paper.
While Momma sat at this small table across from this white lady

Using words like "medicated" and "neglect",
Writing notes in her lil red book, asked me to draw her a pretty picture.
She say "something for your mother, something to depict her".
Whatever that means...
I think she wanna know how much Momma loves me.
Then asked about Grandpa and if Momma still has those bad dreams.
Dreams of when Grandpa use to play doctor, slide her panties off...
And huff and puff on top of her.
She wanted Momma to help me draw the picture but...
Momma rocked back and forth, smoking her cigarette;
Yelling at the lady that, "I don't need this shit!".
And well my picture....I never got to finish it."

She grew, she grew into something I couldn't recognize...
About age 14, I caught her stumbling out of some nigga's ride.
I grabbed her and held her so tight...
Told her "I been praying for you and I know you hurting".
She looked up, shoved me off of her...
And replied, *"Well your prayers ain't working'.*
Grew up and it happened so fast and you can blame it on her momma
For telling Candice, *"Be nice and sit on the man's lap."*
That night turned into every weekend and then...
Mom's boyfriend moved in and it turned into every evening.
Her momma, deaf in her high, can't hear the screaming pass the kitchen.
Life can be so damn vindictive...Candice was drowning within herself;
For being pretty left her all alone in the deep end.

Long ago a daughter lost her mother, I tried to ease her hurt...
They say it's all God's vision, but she seem to see the worst.
Candice, now Candy, a tooth aching oxymoron.
Contrary to never knowing her father but loves her "daddies".
Deeper than the Instagram ass pics and taunts, I just "smdh", "lol',
Double tap my screen; and give her all the attention she wants.
Realizing her future is her mother's past that sits next to her pills,

Next to the devil that got a hex on her ills;
She put her problems in a box beside her lonely times;
Under lock and key, buried deep off in her mind
And when it gets too full, and she can't close the lid
She smokes a blunt, pops a pill, and opens her legs...
And her time spent too often on her back that she couldn't afford.
Long before she knew her body, her momma called her "whore".
So her shame gets baptized in Hennessy...
Regret painted in oxy, and flushed with coke.
She gave up way before she even started...
Well children do what they know.
How she sees herself? Her self she sees no help.
And there ain't no more screaming behind the blinds...
Cause she feels like there's no one to hear her cries.

HEY HOE! Where is the sweet little girl that I use to know?
People often wonder how a hoe becomes a hoe.
I believe it's a destination out of desperation.
This is my attempt to understand...her interpretation.

Iron Stargazer

The Fall:
Her mother was fighting for fear of what may come too early...
Because she bloomed too early too.
So she learned to hold her tears back but the burden was so heavy
That affected other flowers like her aunties and granny.
She grew into a lady from good intensions of her father...
Her eyes are the perfect picture of our youngest daughter.
I thank her mother for this gift of a flower.
I promise to keep her watered, her petals clean and thorns stronger..
With me, she is free, no vas or wire for restricting of leaves.
She is growing and I'm such an admirer of her budding
Becoming sturdy and gorgeous as she wanna be.

The Winter:
I remember she was conflicted, touching the framework..
Of uncertain existence; may the sun kiss her unconditionally.
I love her for the feeling of her heart not the fears of her mind,
The pollution that she use to illuminate such.
Beautiful, the evolution of her bud.
So tell me 'bout your roots, show me the ridges of your truth
As I observe her late summer bloom.
Cause I love her enough for the both of us.
I know she been through more than most of us.
I started with the petal, ended with the stem,
Thinking by my heart, "Damn I never knew love before then".
They say the heart is underneath and guarded in insecurities,
I finally found the key...uunderneath the thorns and leaves.
I see pass the physical which makes her attractive
And focus on the things I can't see in which I'm attracted.
A hold on me and I'd spend forever as her captive.
So baby, let me see you bloom for me.

The Spring:
Over the last season's thoughts, her spirit became so soft.
Her mind's like linen sheets but 3000 counted cloth;
I was told by the showers of the tears dropped.
I held a bright night to a dark mourning and she swooned...
That's her joy from gloom, concrete womb to bloom.
Sweet, soft, naive flower battling an inherited doom.
So a full lady she became through the struggle that never went away.

The Summer:
A wife and a mother, a sister and a daughter, a friend;
I had searched forever for something like her.
They say its two types of pain to mend;
One that only hurts and the other that changes you.
I've seen her go through turmoil to give birth to life.
Mine and our princess too; I pray her own seeds will be able to
Exchange the heavens for a mirror full.
And see themselves as the greatest reflection of God.
Because they became because of her.
Just let me hold her in a dark place...
And when it's cold among the warm trees
I know we both come from hard times.
My soul is aroused how she arose from the concrete.
But not a rose, I know she digs Stargazers...
This love is profound, no one can outweigh us.

Did you hear about the stargazer that grew...
From a crack in the concrete?...It learned to walk without feet.
Said to have no mind but shined by keeping it's dreams.
Through the toxic air, it learned how to breathe.
Long live the stargazer nourished by the unforgiving streets.

Inspired by Tupac Shakur "The Rose that Grew from the Concrete"

Oceans

Well SHIT, that's just how McClain's get along...
Fighting for our rights even when we're wrong.
The ocean's baby, the reef's maybe?..
There was always just the two of us.
We were so much alike that we never appreciated...
That it was just the two of us.
You raised me right with just a handful of hugs.
Covered under our breath professing our love.
Whatever you went through as a kid,
A lot of missed affection when you're the middle of ten.
Still a hero of mine but as an adult, I can now see my parent's sins.
"Son, I'm so proud of you, I'm so proud."
I can't remember ever hearing those words come out ya mouth...
To be rich from time but oh so poor cause of the smallest things.
I know I don't call like I should but I'm anxious...
Cause with enough conversation...
We'll be fighting again...and over the smallest things.

Slipping through my fingers but strong enough to hold up a ship.
And I found myself passing you by on a drift...
You don't know when you're wrong...you must be always right.
Then I'm pissed at you cause I'm a hypocrite.
Turn around and do the same thing with my wife.
I swear we the closest strangers, I swear how close we are estranged us...
Still I made sure to take your shoes off, cover you with a blanket...
When you fell asleep in front of the TV after your second job.
My college days, you'd get angry when I wouldn't come home.
I didn't realize till I was grown that you just wanted me to come home.
I was young and stayed chillin' in my room for growth,
It was so spacious...thought my mouth was quiet,
My mind was like a Trump riot.
Then it just gets worse when I'm in private.

Now most of our arguments through text...
I hope I read that right.
Animosity or not?..shoulda, coulda, got me vexed.
Sperm donor's checks weren't shit and you surpassed making due.
I had no clue what you was goin' through...
How could you be so strong?
And how could I be so selfish, I know I can be so selfish.
You put up with a young me, *"Damn you so selfless."*
So I reach my hand out...but I feel so helpless.
Tried to drown my sorrows BUT THEY LEARNED TO SWIM.
A bit more time, a little bit while longer,
DAMN, I MISS MY BIG MOMMA..
And losing precious seconds of getting to know her daughter.
Corduroy pants and Lacrosse shirts when the first day of school came.
I'll go to my grave with the memory of the sacrifices you made.
Got me right back when them niggas...
Broke in and stole my Nintendo games.
Content with not having everything as long as Saturdays
You had the Keith Sweat playing; incents on roam, fragrance of home.
It's still with me till this day...scrambled eggs and cheese toast.
That expression on your face...was priceless...
That even our distance couldn't push away.

An ocean blue gave birth to me, rippling sapphires shimmering;
But the deepest mystery...coolest Pacific that soothed my soul,
Bluest exhibit could freeze me whole.
Looking up from the bottom's floor, history of these artifacts;
I need to know, this life in her aquarium, to understand...
It's tides, she's tired and burying me beneath her hands.
The ocean, so deep and wide...
And I swim amongst the tears she never let me see her cry...

I LOVE YOU, MOMMA.

Blacker Than

Black, blacker, blackest, black, blacker than blacker than....
Blacker than my feet, barefoot in the summer rain.
Looking at the sky, letting God's tears shower my face.
Blacker than the night of our innocence catching fireflies.
Blacker than the iron eye where Big Momma...
Put so much love in her sweet potato pie.
Blacker than fish fries and Kool-Aid dyes, with little to eat...
Blacker than syrup sandwiches, licking my hands on both sides.
Hey, whatever you can get just to get by.

Word to Gov'ment cheese and cinnamon-sugar toast
Blacker than wearing hand- me- downs from your big brother
That fits like little brother's clothes.
Blacker than running that electric bill sky high
Cause you won't keep Big Momma's screen do' closed.
Blacker than *"GET YO ASS FROM OUT INFRONT OF THE TV!"*
Cause yo Momma ain't no maker of glass.
And Ms. Jenkins from down the street will WHOOP YO ASS!
Then you get home and your momma WHOOP YO ASS...
That's when youngins knew how to act.
Blacker than four corners with four different churches on the same side.
Different religion, same complexion, different opinions,
Same prejudice but it's all division.
Blacker than selling crack out of your momma's $30,000 home;
With your 7 series parked right outside.

That's 15 years in the state pen, picked up 15 times by the age of 15.
That's a convicted felon before 45 that goes back to prison;
Cause that's the only life he's use to living.
The addition is simple;
But we run from mathematics and the school system.
Shit, I never said everything was all right.
It's the elephant in the room created by an explosion in the galaxy;
Bounded all the stars and turned upside down the Moon.
What was once royalty, died young;
Wrapped in gold among a black tomb.
Now my sonogram is a duplicate of fetal poverty in a black womb.
It's hard as hell reading the writings on the wall trapped in a black room.
Black, blacker, blackest, black, blacker than blacker than....

Blacker than a national hero within a country without a history.
Of an orphan, the epitome, of simply existing with stolen liberty;
My momma couldn't protect me.
She did the best she could but even she never knew her ancestry.
This rushing to my 9 year old brain, too proud in my inadequacy in class.
Among the white students with all the answers,
That formulated dreams so minuscule they couldn't
Tiptoe on my taste buds...in a gallery of disappointments
Hanging from nails of hopeless existence;
Drowning in an ocean of "why did this life choose me?".
So I listened...praying heavy to heaven for some understanding...
From the top turnbuckle, wrestling reality hopin' it don't kill us...
But it wasn't until my teens till I ever seen a Black Jesus.
Black, blacker, blackest, black, blacker than black...

Blacker than sleepin' at the foot of the bed...
With your cousin's feet right next to your head.
Blacker than Black Power gibberish, "That don't keep the lights on!"
Black brother, Black brother...Right on, right on!

49

Blacker than breast feeding white babies that will one day be the boss.
Then demanding reparations, they take your life, and give you a holiday.
Blacker than forgetting the meaning and just wanting the day off.
Blacker than watching Roots with Auntie on 17th Street...
On a pallet under the AC unit on a hot summer day.
From having your own originated in a whole other continent...
And now your whole family is Baptist.
Through murder and human trafficking,
Blacker than through the worst, we still thriving!
All these things, the beauty, I couldn't find in.
My nappy hair, big lips, nose is obtuse, my world knew,
Truth eclipsed, I stayed confused; 20 years it took me dig it up...
From under the gravel, twisted manuscript, and dusty shackles.
Facts couldn't stay hidden, A PHARAOHS' ON THE LOOSE!

Saccharine in nature, proof is the centuries of appropriation...
Everything black, but they're afraid of that,
For centuries they've been stealing that.
Some people simply hate black, cause they fear black.
Remember this, every color started from black, just remember that.
I want everything black; well damn, ain't it a lot sweeter like that.
BLACK. BLACKER. BLACKEST...YEEAAAHHH!

Revolution Won't Grow on Trees

FINANCIAL FREEDOM! What your momma told you about but didn't quite know how to do. What your daddy left the house for in hopes to find for himself but never did. What your granddaddy was a laborer all his life for and died with nothing to leave his family. What your big momma prayed so hard for and put extra in the collection plate for while scrubbing floors in hopes to see for her grandchildren and never did. Financial Freedom, it seems so attainable yet simultaneously so far out of reach. With my educational and professional background, I would be remise to not speak to this dilemma within the black community when it means so much to me. I would like to refer you to the beloved and honored Reverend Dr. Martin Luther King Jr for his 5 financial lessons in which some would say was the real reason that he was assassinated.

The passivism could no longer go on fighting the righteous fight once his message began covering economic injustice and the need for a radical redistribution of economic and political power while boycotting some of the biggest industry leaders such as Coca Cola and Wonder Bread. I will also be utilizing an article written by Ebony Financial Blogger, Ms. Lynnette Khalfani-Cox (2014) below to further illustrate the depiction of the ideals of Dr. King and my vision for Black Financial Freedom:

- **1st Lesson:** "Do not wait for economic change; instead create the change." "Freedom is never voluntarily given by the oppressor; it must be demanded by the oppressed."

Complaining about your job, your low pay, replacing your expensive tires, or any other economical "unfair" position that you may drop in your lap will not make it go away. Black folks must be willing to do the work to improve our circumstances and move forward into the remarkable direction that we see for ourselves.

- **2nd Lesson:** "Fight for financial freedom." "There is nothing in all the world greater than freedom....I would rather be a free pauper than a rich slave..." Growing up lower-middle class, it was impressed upon me to go to school, "play by the rules", and get a good job. I wish I would have been taught to create my own entity to produce true wealth so I wouldn't become well educated just to ask someone else for a job.

- **3rd Lesson:** "Step out on faith and take a risk." "Faith is taking the first step even when you can't see the whole staircase." This seems absurd when you have bills to pay but save and work towards leaving that "steady paycheck" for a life of financial freedom. Because we are usually living from paycheck to paycheck, we grow afraid to take the necessary risks that will place us in the right positions for financial freedom. Honestly for myself, formal education and the desire to work in the corporate arena, has made me into an "educated coward".

- **4th Lesson:** "Your education, job, or career status does not define you." "Everybody can be great...because anybody can serve...You only need a heart full of grace. A soul generated by love." Do not allow your outlook to be clouded by your title or your degree, or the lack of either. Dr. King reminded us all that we can go as far as our faith and hard work will take us. Also, Black folks should not permit a job to affect our inner peace.

- **5th Lesson:** "Take your work seriously." "If a man is called to be a street sweeper, he should sweep streets even as Michelangelo painted, or Beethoven composed music or Shakespeare wrote poetry." Even though Dr. King taught us that we are not defined by our careers, I really dig that he nevertheless advised to take your job and your calling in life seriously. He advocated that no matter how exalted or how common your profession, you should execute with honor and pride.

This hard work, risk taking, higher sense of self, and execution is in essence not for you at all. The fruits of your labor are for your children. I was once told that to send your brood of your loins to college just to become great employees is downright criminal and a form of modern day slavery. The most influential people, the ones who leave behind incredible legacies, will live on in the hearts of the people they touch. We, Black folks, do not operate within the concept of true community, generational wealth, and leaving a lasting legacy. White people send their kids to college to simply solidify their industry market value and when they graduate, they hand them a high paying career. Asians establish whole sectors of a city with their own establishments through hard work and vigilant savings and investments. This practice enables them to provide employment and true ownership by adulthood. They also teach their children the actual business practices during their adolescence. Black folks usually leave debt, an expensive funeral bill, and a lack of knowledge to be foraged unto the multitudes of failure and in this instance, empty soliloquies of "find it out on your own". Instead, principles, philosophies and achievements should become immortal, spreading from generation to generation.

What will you be known for when you leave this earth? To tell a Black man in this nation, from his own or any other group of people, to lift themselves up by their own bootstraps is absolutely asinine. America has enabled, trained, fed, and brought technological advances to so many other impoverished peoples and countries that just happened to look nothing like the Black man. I say that to say, nobody else can do this, no document can do this, and no emancipation proclamation can bring financial freedom and financial literacy to our people but us. To free ourselves and become financial beings with a mindset surrounding legacy, true wealth, and inherited knowledge as strategic means to a "mountain top" end. "It is all about the money", this is the mindset in which we are reared with. Nonetheless we must learn that being rich is not the goal but instead to become wealthy, learn to budget, accrue ownership, and have something to pass on to our children. That will be the portion manifested to life from the depths of "The Dream" that America does not like to recite on dear MLK Day. Though the sentiment would lead to the real revolution for us Black folks that we have been oh so waiting on.

LET'S GET FREE.

Nigger Rich

THIS IS FOR THE NIGGER IN YOU.

The Ignorant Bliss:
GOD AIN'T COMIN' BACK!
Somebody tell them Christians that it's Nevuary...
And my 40 acres and mule is a necessary.
I filed early so my return coming late February.
I can't wait for these rainbow colored diamonds,
All flavors mixed, like Ben & Jerry's.
My baby momma lost her reparations in a handbag.
We together for the kids and family pics,
All for IG with a tax refund hash tag.
Never met a nah-notha-nigga this hot, worthless stones in a bezzle,
Big ass gaudy wrist watch.
Just added 3 more kids to the dependent column,
I say I'm ballin', all sweet like Jason Collins.
Then I spent $400 bucks on this...
Just to post and caption *"NIGGA, YOU AIN'T UP ON THIS!"*
Lookin' just like a mansion with the projects behind it.
Bought 5 pair of Jordan 11's, a 93' Lexus...with a bad transmission,
Pink sprinkles in my lady's up-do trailed by 10 pounds of weave...
And 26's on the CANDY COATED BOX CHEVY!
This had to be what Dr. King meant for me.
Trunk BOOM like a damn stampede,
In your living room from the damn street...
You don't have to listen closely to hear my American Dream.

Money dance, do the money dance.
This the ignorant shit you like, hot damn!

The Entertained Hegemony:
Here ye, here ye, come and watch all these niggas...
Who ain't ever had money;
Let the Nigger Holiday commence, annual tax season.
The most money any of these niggas done seen and...
Performing phenomenal feats that you wouldn't believe.
Making millions of dollars disappear in the matter of weeks.
While behind in rent, stuntin' in foreign boutiques.
Hit the mall and cop everything they see;
From the liquor store to the local swap meet.
Plenty spent for the Asians, Hispanics, Persians,
And the Irish see that these niggas love to drink.
"Brotha, Brotha, open your eyes, and see the bigger picture!"
"Nigga, I got the 85 inch, I can't get any bigger or clearer!"...
Financial independence will be their real freedom
But they rather be Toby with a buying power up to $1 Trillion.
Cause Kunta is too much hurt and we know them niggas hate to work.

Money dance, do the money dance.
This the ignorant shit you like, hot damn!

The Black Woke:
People say money ain't everything;
What about ownership? Well most of us ain't owning shit!
So either dope dealing or slanging a 9 to 5,
The white man gettin' paid off both of those highs.
Now niggas can't make it to ballots to choose leadership;
But we can make it to Apple or the latest LeBron release...
So we're on fleek with a commander and chief...
With a spray tan, bad toupee, and white nationalists beliefs.
Monopolies on poverty, we're slave ship dock bound.

CASH RULES EVERYTHING AROUND THESE NIGGAS!
As pride and dignity around me wither.
Rich can play broke forever, nigga but broke, can't play rich for long.
Hither you can be Chicken George or a John Waller figure,
The master or the slave but nowhere in the middle.
Blinded by the bread but you too focused on the crumbs, nigga...
I don't know when we decided that it was cool...to be a dumb nigga.

HAPPY TAX SEASON, NIGGERS!

Prototype

GOD IS WOMAN! YES, GOD HAS TO BE A WOMAN!
How else did the world become so beautiful yet vengeful?
What a gorgeous - phenomenal piece of blasphemy, right?...

So dangerous that the male ego re-wrote human society
Many times over cause of the notion but let's be honest...
How can we blame Eve when history has shown...
That women NEVER KNOW what they want to eat!
The conclusion, you must be the "prototype" of what God should be.

And this "Prototype", I had to learn how to live with...
At age 7, frustrated, I pushed a pretty curly haired girl
Named Michelle down on the playground.
Michelle told the teacher, the teacher told my Momma,
And I GOT MY ASS BEAT...first time a woman's words ever hurt me.
At age 10, my first love was Vanity from The Last Dragon.
If she would've showed me her moves...
I SHO-NUFF! could've worn that tight ass yellow suite.
The first time a woman never knew I existed but had my heart.
The closest thing to God YET WE CALL YOU A BITCH.
In my early teens I had a bad habit of this.
Maybe Too Short was to blame, definitely not how I was raised.
Though I never said it to your face...
First time I realized that even my thoughts could disrespect you.
And at age 15, I swear you were always in my dreams.
Shipwrecked, crystal clear turquoise made it transparent for me.
To the bottom of the ocean floor, colors of the coral reef...
Looked like the flyest floral piece.
You smiled and I became instantly infatuated...so I often stayed
In that beautiful adolescence and woke up confused in a wet paradise.
YEA, YOU MUST BE THE PROTOTYPE...

No tan or curved enhancement, just amazing roads.
May I put my hands in your complexion and play in your street,
The one less traveled; shall I find comfort at every stop.
So damn perfect yet your eyes only learned to see the flaws in yourself.

You never get to view how you light up when you laugh
Or how beautifully you hold our daughters when they cry.
BUT ALLOW ME TO AWAKEN, YOU QUEEN!
Those stretch marks are extraordinarily illustrated...
From bringing life into this world.
Your hair is thick as a replication of your soul; bends but shall not break.
That lil pudge is just more to love, your thighs touch too much...
Cause they golden gate an outside of this world treasure.
So all confines, borders, and restraints are a must.
PERFECTION...and I do not use this word lightly.
I use it so heavy to paint your reflection that my heart beats to.
I use it to write a million poems for a million days speaking
Eloquently on your behalf but for mere seconds...
I use the word so heavy in fact, so PROFOUND when I speak of you...
That I am now a power lifter, the STRONGEST MAN ON EARTH.
See, I told you that you'd make me better.
If anything, woman, YOU ARE TOO PERFECT!

I often think that people have NEVER BEEN IN LOVE
When they seem to NEVER HAVE ENOUGH TO FIGHT FOR.
How beautiful it has been that I warred and fell...
Deep into this unknown place and dwelled for the past decade.
In a land where love had a face and a full name.
I was able to walk up to Love, graze her elbow to get her attention.
A bit nervous for this first encounter, cleared my throat to ask,
"Can I have you forever?"...and then you said *"I do"*...

YES QUEEN, I KNOW THAT YOU MUST BE.

Inspired by Outkast "Prototype" (2003)

The Day After

The first time you see her. The first time you've ever seen him. The feeling of the "new new" chase. The sexiness between every slight touch, every side glance. This must be one of a kind type of manifestation or infatuation that you've found and you have to indulge. The new taste, the new touch, the new feeling against your pelvic wanting a closer feel pass the pores that are already as close as they could ever be but all to what extent?

I was so damn scared of just the thought of telling my Mom I was going to be a teenage father that when I first started having sex at the tender age of 15, I used condoms and even went as far as pulling out to watch my little soldiers march into the 98% effectiveness of the Trojan wrapping security. I was not taking any chances. Honestly, most of my peers including myself rarely thought about STDs but instead worried about the possibility of being a father. Smart, right? Years passed and the onslaught of college women caught more than my eye, third eye included, one eyed snake, whatever you would like to call it. The scare of disappointing or angering my Moms from my dorm room or college apartment had left my consciousness and I had become a martyr of my loins and somehow unprotected sex became a habitual occurrence for me.

"I don't give a shit about givin it up on the first night/ That just let me know she know what she want.../ She so god damn sweet, sweet as she wanna be/ Oo I just like Oo I wanna lay in her hair.../ Maybe I'll just roll over and just lay on her booty." – Andre 3K "Where's My Panties Interlude"

Waking up to something like a stranger can definitely be frightening but the sensations became so familiar and I was addicted. The "wet wet", how strong the pull, how intense the sensations the bodies make converging into one another...with no boundaries...latex boundaries to be exact. I know we have all been there. Ignoring the desire to stop to grab protection but instead groping one another in a restaurant bathroom, against the wall, over a table, under a playground slide (ya'll nasty), or just good ol drunk missionary in your best friend's bedroom. So mighty fine, don't you agree? But the next morning comes, it never fails, the morning after will always be there. The next morning will come and now the liquor has left you and been replaced with a headache on top of the reluctance to lift up the covers. "Who is lying next to you?" is the new adventure on an early Sunday morning. I immediately went into my session of regrets and prayers to the Lord that I would never do anything like this again if this young lady was not impregnated. I'm sure the Lord thought this prayer was on repeat because it was frequently replayed like a skipping record. Then comes the resolve, the Day After pill.

The day after pill was my "go to" so I continued on this destructive path and even then the fear of children had me sick to my stomach. Fifty dollars to continue to go "raw" was a small sacrifice for my indulgence. I would seriously get the sweats and "the shits" for days awaiting the "all clear' text. This path went on and off until my mid 20s and then finally perspective set in. A perspective that now focused on the children's lives that I ended after those nights of reckless abandonment. The feeling still haunts me to this day and I count my blessings when I look into my two daughter's eyes. A feeling I couldn't have ever imagined – when my wife first showed me the pregnancy test that showed me God was shining on me in favor and I was going to be a father. No sweats, no irritableness, no regret. I was a married man and about to be a father. I had an enormous sense of pride that I was bringing a life into this world but now under the foundation of marriage. The appreciation for life and the sense of responsibility was now eclipsed over what use to be....My "Day After".

Fire & Desire

"It was pain before pleasure...Then you showed me what a love could do (Woo, hoo)...Fire and desire...Fire and desire...Feelin' good to you."

"Baby, I'm coming to BREAK YO ASS OFF!" is what she said...

Somebody told me that this planet was small then...
I found my soul mate in the moonlight of a dance hall.
Lying to our spouses and we followed the protocol...
When I ordered "My Stranger's" favorite of Hennessy and Coke.
Against her cheek, I rubbed a single rose.
On the dance floor with saxophones,
My hands, couldn't control themselves, our feet gliding like jazz
Instrumentals among a room full of silhouettes.
Caressing her to the bottom of her spine, snares drumming as I kissed
Her neck, my lips on the horns of seduction,
Our minds, to a place more simple onlookers to see.
We could be compromised but the moment, we thought,
Was worthwhile to jeopardize as our frontal lobe was monopolized,
I understood her pain from being a troubled child.
She saw my unmet need to be appreciated from a mile away,
And I was told diamonds can be found in the harshest hues,
As I seduce, for that night, she was my muse,
My woman at home couldn't stop me so I continued
And "My Stranger's" ring never stopped her...
Then we headed up to our favorite room and this occurred...

"Baby, I'm coming to BREAK YO ASS OFF!"...
Is what she told me...to disguise, I headed up before soon after,
A knock on the door I opened it to an untied trench coat.
Rain painted her breast and the single rose the night was still young,
So I took her coat off slow.
We knew it was wrong, we can't explain why,
I'm wondering how he functions with heaven between her thighs.
He's a good provider but he touches her less...
Is it 'cause she married too young or that my wife never listens to me?
She knows what she wants and don't mind tellin' me...

65

But does her husband know the same?
Honestly I too could be to blame so our goal...
Was to make a mess of the sheets for the maid.
To the couch she went and bent it over,
Made it clap a lil, looked back, and then winked.
I had a clear view through her lingerie with her heels on,
I lifted her off her feet then down to her knees.
Feeding her inner needs from starvation,
She threw her back against the wall.
Well pedicured toes reaching for the ceiling.
Breaking her inhibitions was the heist,
Thrusting her desires to new heights.
I would throw her remorse to the stars to rip the sky to free fall into
Two lovers that shouldn't be but can't deny.

Just by breathing on her brain, I made her shiver,
Slid my hard ambition inside of her drowning condition
Rushing back down to drink my addiction,
She's moving so delicious like we're making motion pictures.
Yearning to relapse from a bottomless place...
While Keith Sweat "Young But You're Ready" plays.
She leaned back on this ride and drove her stress away.
Revisiting a previous stage, we continued to perform our reservations.
She asked, *"Whose is it, Daddy?"* with no remorse.
But these drunk answers were the truth...
Ownership is who your heart belongs to.

We leave each other in the deep of the night,
Driving back to our trusting spouses.
She reached her front door, I went through my back passing family
Photos of when my wife had young aspirations.
She saw pictures of when he took more time when she felt strange,
Seeing her body change bringing new life.

Both of us was never quick to forgive, I learned my spouse was never
Meant to be fixed and grasped **the smallest piece**...
I hesitantly slid into my wife's sheets.
She turned to her husband to kiss him goodnight.
I turned toward my wife to do the same.
I kissed "My Stranger" and smiled for our secrets.
And held one another for we enjoyed the night...
Where we once again found one another.

Inspired by Rick James & Teena Marie "Fire and Desire" (1981)

Woman, Thou Art

"When Eve was brought unto Adam, he called her simply "mother" of all In this consists the glory and the most precious ornament of woman."...

This is for the queen that gave me life.
The mother of the church, that never spares the rod...
And Oh how hard she works for God.
For the entire sea of mahogany rainbow skin queens.
For the frustrated woman fed up with life.
For the woman racially mixed and never knew who to identify with.
And the mother of the mother whose daughter gave me life,
That every day put one foot in front of the other.
The woman corner store hustling food stamps,
.50 cent on the dollar pushing quarter waters.
For the woman who raises her family by her lonesome
With worries holding her blood pressure so tight...
But smiles for her children so bright.
You are the physical form of what God's love must look like.
For the woman with Afro-centric shouts and hair,
Dashiki clothed, Massai pride beads, and Sankofa visions in her eyes.
The woman - old school use to double dutch in her Keds
With a back pocket full of Jacks and Chico legs;
Sliding on a cardboard box with a Roy Rodgers & Dale Evans lunchbox.
For the one carrying a suitcase, perm pressed hair, and corporate walk..
Because the bills need paying and she assumed...
Time ran out on her dream's clock.
For the woman that praises but is not defined by her complexion's tone...
You are all more than worldly but we call you our own.

For the woman dressed in pink today...
That couldn't fight her genetics, lost her mother from the same ailment.
Still views herself as beautiful without her hair or breast.
Grabbing on to victory through the pain
And when she is weary and body is worn...
Like hundreds of hours on top of hundreds of days
That have been beating her down more than hundreds of ways.
She still makes it through somehow.

Instead of holding on to old memories she still fights to make new ones.
And she keeps picking herself back up because..
Chemo keeps beating her back down.
She sees freedom from this darkness;
Becoming a stranger by the mirror but she knows
This survivor all too well.
Choosing what she thinks, how she loves, and knowing no fear.
Her spirit is more immense than this earth's body and she knows...
If need be she will leave it here.
But she will never surrender because SHE IS WOMAN.
Our mother, sister, wife, cousin, daughter, best friend.
She is woman and she is everything.

"You are everything...and everything is you...
Oh, you are everything...and everything is you...
'Cause you are everything...and everything is you."

Inspired by The Stylistics "You Are Everything" (1971)

The Token Blackie
(Mask Off)

During a late night movie, I nervously looked around for witnesses. I rushed the drive-thru girl for our food and then snuck my guest into my empty college apartment. I turned the TV on to "Living Single" and she asked to turn it to "Friends". I said, "Yea, it's cool" because I was counting down the minutes to remove her clothes anyway. About an hour later, she laid next to me and rubbed my well brushed waved fade and exclaimed, "Wow, Cordney I just love your hair". She then went on to give me what I felt was meaningless compliments until she uttered words like "boyfriend", "relationship", and "situation". And then she said, "You know Cordney, you're nothing like the other black guys I've been with". Then the expression "Bitch, WHAT?!" fumbled out of my mouth.

"They take me to the back and pat me/ Askin' me about some khakis/ But let some black people walk in/ I bet they show off their token blackie" – Kanye West "Spaceship" (2004)

They, as in white people, to not be misunderstood with any other "theys", do not want to see a nigga at their job. The above mentioned occurrence was the first time I made the connection that I was living in white society navigating well through social nuances because I was able to contort my "mask" for situational conformity. In laymen's terms, I was "tap dancing for the white man". Maybe this was done subconsciously but it was assimilation none the less while becoming lost in a "double consciousness". A concept that Mr. W. E. B. Du Bois first explored in 1903 publication, "The Souls of Black Folk".

Double Consciousness is described as the individual sensation that your identity is of several parts, making it almost impossible to have one cohesive self. This theory stated that one's self-perception is damaged and unable to embrace one's own uniqueness and instead may judge said person's self as the outside world would or the white world in this case. This perception makes it extremely hard for blacks to succeed in many arenas but I have been a witness within Corporate America. I stay quiet during promotion time, work hard in hopes of recognition, and keep my mouth closed in fear of any unwarranted disciplinary action. I hold on for dear life if my miniscule position is threatened because I have been brainwashed to believe this is as good as it gets for me, for us, "po' black folk".

I have been in Corporate America for an accumulative amount of 15 years. Among that time I had either been the only black man, and many times, the only black person, at the company, branch, or department where I was employed. The dilemma about being the only black person in the office is that it comes with the responsibility of destroying or reaffirming all of the stereotypes and also becoming the office' book of knowledge on all things "black". Though, the extent of these interactions will be largely determined by their comfort level and acceptance which are equated with: if I fit in, am reliable, trouble for their department, or if I am a "team player" whatever definition they hold for that term. The real question is: can he "play his role" and be the "token" for us?

The phenomenon of the "token" black employee is still alive and well and I have been playing this role among other "edu-ma-cated" black professionals since I made straight A's and a teacher saw some type of "magnificent potential" among the rest of the "simple negroes". This is why as a black educated man I have done okay in Corporate America. I, for the most part, fit a particular profile: educated, articulate, somewhat cultured, and perhaps non-threatening depending on the ideals of the executives.

When these characteristics are on full display, they contribute to the comfort level of whites. But know this white people; I am in your office, fully aware of all of this and am aware that you are aware of this too. I, black people, want a fair shake and have been working twice as hard to achieve the same success. I have never wanted any sympathy for the way things are. Similar to what Jackie Robinson was asking for, I just want to be able to play on the same damn field....and in doing so TAKE MY MASK OFF.

Don't Wanna Go

Slave master asked for my letter, I pledged, and he handed me a rifle.
I knew what it meant until I thought to never see my family again...

My commander said, "*I'm so pleased to hear that you volunteered*".
I'm wondering...WHO THE HELL LIED TO HER?
Let me stay here and fight for people who look like me
Against the persecution because they look like me.
Isis? Shit, I don't even know them people.
I wear the uniform and understand what comes with it
But autocratic bigotry painted as democracy...
They can travel overseas and not take me with it.
Words to live by or die to, if I die in that other land,
I doubt my family will understand.
They won't sing the National Anthem a bit harder
Or pledge the flag a little longer...
"*HE DIED FOR OUR FREEDOMS!*"
How dumb does that shit really sound?...
When Jerome gets one hundred years for an ounce
And Sandra gets mysteriously "found"...
Within the confines of a secured jailhouse.
I believe they'll say, "He shouldn't been there in the first place....
When our worth in this free country can't even value his face."

Tell my babies, "*Daddy has to go far, far away*".
Kiss my wife and see that hurt in her face.
For a nation that doesn't love me or you.
Staring at a land unfamiliar daydreaming of their laughter.
Insomnia at night because I can't kiss them goodnight.
Dismissing my pain for America's crimes, missing my daughter's
First times, watching mirages of manifested milestones.
HELL NO! I don't wanna leave...HELL NO! I don't wanna go!
While Flint still dying from toxic H2O! Flint still dying from toxic H2O!
Police water cannons on brown people...

Modern day Standing Rock or Birmingham in 64', pipeline protesting.
I guess the First Amendment only works for Fox News and white people.
No cell phones, this documented by drone videos within a great nation..
Priding itself on humanitarian idioms,
The Government requesting disclosure from citizens is like hearing...
"If you find cancer don't tell me" from a patient,
They really don't want to hear about their symptoms or the cure.
Reluctantly, we're volun-told to contribute to the ends of the pages.
To kill brown people with my brown face is...
Exactly what Uncle Sam wants to read as the prefaces.

HELL NO! I don't wanna go...HELL NO! I don't wanna leave!
HELL NO! I don't wanna go...HELL NO! I don't wanna leave!
And walk away from the people I love...
FOR A COUNTRY WHO NEVER LOVED ME.

Rain On Me

"Raindrops...Raindrops...Raindrops keep falling on my head.
Fallin', fallin', fallin' on my head, they keep fallin'..."

Digging through years to bury my "Baby Boy" sense,
Someone had to be praying for I found where my Taraji is.
Now I learn from toddlers cause at 2 and 1, nothings bothering them.
While adults make dyer of the things we cannot touch...
Amongst the storms, please give them the bluest of skies.
Fluff their clouds like pillows to comfort their slumber.
Steal the thunder, dim it, and turn it into lullabies.
As I dodge the news, the "piercing reminder" that in 2017,
Anatomy could still murder their father,
Slice the throat of his culture, let my diaspora bleed.
Load up and mend the borders cause a tweet may start World War III.

"So I just did me some talking to the sun.
Told em' I didn't like the way he got things done."

But for today, enjoy the rain, my Loves.
You see those good people in khakis waving NAZI flags?
While I stand here with ruffled wings on the battlefield of time...
The field has my blood in the soil but it was never mine.
Gridiron or cotton, clock ticks much faster living off of borrowed time.
When tired and forgotten, I don't even debate anymore.
It's like begging for empathy from worthless tears of blind eyes...
On night schemes that become daydreams that'll never be seen
By you or I, well at least not in this lifetime.
So jump in the biggest puddles, let rain swim down your innocent face.
May it kiss you in the most gentle of ways.
For today, my princesses, enjoy the rain.

Beating on the pavement to cool the burn.
I open Facebook to see "new" concerns of our Tango colored chief.
He wants to take some "dreamers" away and push them
Back to a country they ain't ever even seen.
While he lives the dream that was built on the backs of black folk.
"ARE WE EQUAL YET...ARE WE EQUAL YET?"
My babies will ask just that...
With their tiny hands over hearts of a kindergarten class;
Pledging allegiance to a symbol that has only oppressed.
Then the oppressor tells the oppressed the correct way to protest fact.
Reason I don't blame the old or the youngins' no mo'.
It be what they be taught, beige perspective deaded the ROOTS'.
"Things Fall Apart" cause they never knew Black Thought.
But for today, my Loves, today simply enjoy the rain.

"Crying's not for me, 'cause, I'm never gonna stop the rain,
By complaining. Because I'm free, nothing's worrying me."

Inspired by B.J. Thomas "Raindrops Keep Fallin' on My Head" (1969)

Daddy's Lil Soldier

I WILL, I WILL, FIGHT THE HARDEST WARS...
HE PREPARED ME FOR THESE STORMS.
I learned to battle without a gun; I guess his absence was my weapon.

My cries, the deepest thoughts of a mime.
Without boy scouts you helped me build that fire.
Years of basic training and hurtful patches earned.
Sorrow sewn in the upper chest,
Inability for relationships on the lower breast.
Insensitivity on the middle of my arms,
Anger patch hemmed covering my heart.
Omission stitching over my vision at this marine...
With my manhood trying to harbor hiding beneath all this armor.
An abusive pops, beating my emotions while missing in action.
Grew the attraction, Momma fought the chain reaction.
That divided us, a common fraction that became the distraction.
DO YOU REMEMBER THIS TENDER BOY...
That you turned into a rigid soldier?
Now look at your son prepared for military-ism.
I have the vivid images that afflict him, restrict him.
Another martyred convicted victim...
SO WHAT IS THIS BOY'S SILENCE CRYING OUT FOR?...

I could hear the bombs going off amongst the blood, dirt, and the fog.
Helicopter vultures picking off exhausted wild hogs.
Hiking through a red sea, brain buckets littered full of memories.
Ground shaking under my boots up to my knees.
Beneath the trees, a haunting darkness, owl eyes, trigger finger shivering;
The sound of my footsteps startling.
Walking in Lucifer's garden, I can hear em' snarling.
Lying under carnage, not yet a carcass; I step toward the scream of a boy.
His fatigue looked like mine...holding him close,

As we lay in a pool of blood.
"It's going to be okay", were the only words I could utter.
His body limp and limbs with holes in the deep of humidity.
He becomes cold in the abyss of this black jungle; we're all alone.
His gasping is now faint, he reaches for a closer embrace...
That conflicts with his last breath.
He begins talking with Death, yet a peace so out of place;
Just the quiet of the most touching farewell.
His soul leaving this space, I removed his helmet and paused.
Like I crawled outside of my body and my expression seemed erased....
ME AND THIS BOY HAD THE SAME FACE.

Daddy's Lil Soldier.

People Watching II

To the heavens, bright lights in the midst of clouds and then…
Feels likes nobody understands me like him…
Though he can't express himself, a speech impediment.
So I speak for him, using outside voices on the inside;
Showing many of my passed friends and family love
Pouring a little Crown in the ground, spreading love above
When the liquor evaporates to the clouds.
Reminiscence of times that I could feel God touching him.
Too early check-in for that upper room;
Our brother, Paul dressed in all black stomping at the golden gates.
Still having nightmares of that night;
Bullets rang through the hotel suite entering the chest of my friend.
THIS EARTH LACKING YET ANOTHER YOUNG HEARTBEAT.
And selfishly, my guardian angel must've been standing right next to me.
Cause the girl I was dancing with knocked me off my feet;
A stray bullet went through her face and out the back of her cheek.
Her blood soaking him, I heard our Momma's voice whispering,
"Son, trust in him." I saw a light and started pleading for the Lord..
To not let him in and God didn't…
Instead he sent us to group counseling to become better men.
But that didn't the stop Kruger from stalkin' me...

I'M DEMANDING ANSWERS FROM THE LORD!
"WHY!"...When Ashlee "the Great" went home.
Grace and polished of an old soul inside a cosmic youth...
If she was ever caged then he wouldn't have ever known.
But sometimes it was a beautiful pain in her tone
That I took a dive in, a symphonic voice that left footprints on my heart...
In her old Chucks, pink bubble jacket,
And hair and the day's star in sync.
Dear Song Bird, she were a strainer for the Lord
He shined right through anytime she began to pour.
Wings never saw clips and feet were never tied.
It hurt him so much when she had to go live in the sky.

SO I SPOKE TO GOD, FEELING LIKE HIS CHILD AGAIN...

When my grandmother passed as his eyes fill up.
I'm grown now but in the bed still curled up,
Fetal position, wishing Grandma would lift him up.
These days I can't wake up to a dry pillow.
The pain of her loss WON'T LET HIM LET GO.
Heaven treating her like a bus station, my life just passing her by now.
He'll have to tell my kids bout' her like a legend cause they'll never feel
The blessing of my grandmother's affection.
With the throbbing wound of her absence, going insane;
Straight jacket myself because I'd rather be gone...
So she can hold him again.
We was tighter than two brothers with different fathers but yes,
The same mother...this world don't love us, looking in the mirror
To register, waiting for a change.
Well he is just a soul whose intentions are good.
Lord, he is me and I am him...so please don't let us be misunderstood.

People Watching.

On His Way Home

"THOSE FUCKIN' PIGS MURDERED MY BABY!"
- Black Mothers All Over America

Oklahoma Army National Guard veteran with a master's degree...
Leaves two small children and a wife behind...
From the sky, streetlights on his body outlined,
Lying on the ground with a bullet in his heart.
Eyes staring into space, two bullets in his back.
Reported that he was resisting, street painted with his blood;
Wallet in his hand, mistaken for a gun.
"The police questioned where was he coming from..
Then fought him to the ground then they shouted for ID,
He reached for his wallet while restrained...
Then the officer just unloaded his rounds", said by eyewitness.

My heart, my child, cause I can still see your smile...
I have not seen a single sunrise; these flowers can't warm my heart...
When I'm the one who asked him to go to the store.
I told him to be safe; he smiled and said "Momma, of course".
Then for the last time, he walked out my door.
Smiled his last smile to me, laughed his last laugh and I felt his last hug.
I never thought it would be me havin' to bury my son.
A MOTHER SHOULD NEVER HAVE TO BUY THAT COFFIN!
I pray to God that he didn't suffer...
Damn it! This has to be some dream!
Lord, how can the news read so generically...
Like they never knew he had dreams?
Just another black body but I still have flashes of memories...
To times he was a little boy and ran to squeeze my leg;
To now becoming a stereotype, judged and now dead?

This was not what I had planned, a mother can't understand...
I replayed the coverage over and over again in my mind,

I couldn't tell if the scream I was hearing was my son's or mine.
And praying that I could reverse the time to tell him...
Not "If you can't find something to live for" but instead...
"Do all you can do to stay alive" just so I can hold him again.
And if the system has you on your knees
"Then no matter what, them white folks is always right...
Promise Momma, you'll keep your hands in sight...
And bow willingly until you dig a hole in the street."
Just so I could hold him close and feel my cheek against his cheek.

I blinked and the judge yelled for order...
The Court reporter makin' my words shorter.
Though she couldn't interpret the lies in the room's aura.
Next to my son's lawyer, an empty chair, where he should've been.
I went in and out of despair and anger while the officer used his lies..
For protecting him as they read back his confession.
They never found my son with a weapon because there was not one.
They neglected the witness's cell phone footage,
They rejected, admissible was only my own testifyin' and cryin'.
Pleading for a conviction of a wrongful death.
Experts couldn't definitely identify his last breath;
But I knew his voice better than anyone else.

The court awaited as the foreman got the verdict from the bailiff.
I had no more energy for outbursts just tears...
And smeared makeup, stated he was only charged with manslaughter.
All the hope I had collapsed and I fell to the floor.
Up to that moment I had asked the Lord for faith and courage
And bravery but I didn't want to live,
And for courage, I didn't want it no more.

The police killed a son, a husband, and a father.

A 1 year sentence for giving a lifetime to 2 fatherless daughters.

I tell you that I cry sometimes, I cry sometimes...

My heart, my child, cause I can still see your smile.

I can't help but think of you; sometimes I catch a glimpse of you.

So I keep the porch light on...

Hoping you're on your way...on your way home.

And the Winner Is....

DEAR WHITE PEOPLE...and lost ass Black Folk, pardon me from your deep sense of malice and social injustice garnished with confederate flags, red elephants, and truck bumpers covered in your misguided beliefs. I just wanted to give my congrats.

"The voting booth is white people's subconscious!" In the comfort of their private section, behind the curtain, their true feelings manifest themselves without public ridicule. We've had our differences over the past two years. That's probably an understatement. It's true that I wish you hadn't voted the way you did but I don't believe you are bad people. I don't believe you are monsters. I know that most of you are definitely not. You have commented on photos of my daughters and I've pressed the "love" button on your job promotions and inspirational quotes. You've applauded me when things are going well for me and you've offered your condolences during my times of anguish. You have provided a sense of community for me, even if it is the social media kind. BUT WHAT THE HELL WERE YOU THINKIN'?

I really want to believe that you voted the way you did because you worry about the same things I do: protecting your children, supporting your family, secure employment, quality healthcare, good schools, and the confirmation that your future will be just fine. I would pray that you voted for Trump because you want change, because you don't feel like the current world we live in is working. I can't help not to overlook that the hardcore Trump supporters are poor white people who rally the racist-classist misogynist attitude that he carries himself with.

"ATLEAST HE AIN'T NO NIGGER!" is the sensation that I feel when YOU praise this man. With actions such as the movement of people of color from America, placing billionaires with questionable backgrounds in the cabinet, destroying affordable health care with no plan for the future, and the suspicious activities such as the dismissal of Russian interference and the firing of FBI investigator. Then the Charleston response was simply a disgrace for the "Leader of the Free world". All of this while tweeting detestable-degrading-insensitive posts 24-7. We might not agree on policies but I would think we would agree on decency. From a bigotry/racism point of view, this election has shown just how much hasn't changed in the last 50 years. White folks voted for a president that ran off of divisiveness, sexism, and racism but it will be a complete force that ensures that people like Trump that surely desires the rich to keep getting rich and the poor to stay exactly where they are to not triumph over love and decency. And from a federal government point of view, I don't think anything will change. I once heard, "what I look like asking the devil for a blessing?"

From the people that show me so much love within my social media community to the melanin disadvantaged at my place of employment who are so kind in my face but are damn near clansmen on line, we will both not win while this man is in office.

WHAT THE HELL WERE YOU THINKING?

The Bigot in Me

I think I'm starting to understand how to stereotype.

LOCK your doors, CLUTCH your purse when a dark brotha walks by.
"He doesn't look like he's from round here."
But I can't blame you, it's what TV shows what a criminal looks like.
Over or under qualified, darn this muddy pigment of mine.
Loud, ghetto, violent, angry, late, and lazy.
Oh and I never stick around for the babies.
Run fast, jump high, broad nose, sex crazed...
Big, strong buck with a little small brain.
I mean WHO ARE WE TO BLAME?
When "boring" is...Kendrick and Jermaine?
Then we praise one hundred Lil Waynes.
Our violent ways we can't deny...
When Mixon and Rice beat women for internet sites.
WORLDSTAR!..
Displays how we adore to fight and black on black crime...
Is on a 30 year high, I can understand why my suite and tie
And degrees won't let my wicked side hide...
I think I'm learning how to stereotype...

MY GOD, the country had a BLACK PRESIDENT for goodness sakes!
They gave us a pass for almost a decade;
How racist can our country really be?

A topsy-turvy mentality with race versus race we have come to inhabit.
But it's not so racist when people with color have it? hmmm...
That doesn't seem fair at all.
THER IS NO WHITE POWER CONSPIRACY.
Since we so capable and Black Lives Matter has to be a racist attack;
To make whites leave the table, reverse sit-ins now, right?..
Eye for an eye makes everyone blind and slavery...
Well that happened so far back in time.
Your ancestors had no slave owner ties...
I must just walk around with too much race on my mind.
I should convert to keepin' up with the times...
When tan toupee politicians just state whatever's on their minds.
And it's a little offensive but at least he says whatever's on his mind.
Right? And he doesn't have KKK ties they just think a lot alike.
You know, I think I'm learning how to stereotype.

Reason most of us and insecure white liberals are convinced...
That all opposition to Obama is all about race, nothing of his politics.
His dictatorial ways, constitutional dismay or US nuclear secret betray...
Republicans just request his birth certificate for a keeps sake,
Well, Pete's sake"...I think I'm learning how to stereotype.
Understand these are ALL just imaginary.
Black problems!...like old time race riots and long ago lynch mobs.
I'm starting to see it all from the cleared fob;
Like when I see a white boy waving a Confederate flag , in hunting gear,
With muddy tires, praising Limbaugh and the glory days of Bush...
And Reagan in a big truck with John Deere camouflage.
A case of Budweiser riding shotgun with a rifle in the back window;
That must be licensed cause he never gets randomly stopped.
But he looks just like so-n-so that had that black church shot up.
Or the "troubled youth" that raped all those black girls
Then was peacefully walked out by the cops.

But I swear I have plenty of white friends that look just like him.
Man I swear they look just like him...
The stereotype can't be racist if it looks just like him?...
And watermelon and fried chicken are some of my favorites...
Is the world more complex than the stereotype suggests?
The problem isn't that it's inaccurate, maybe that it's incomplete?
Because I'm starting to make some sense of all this blind imagery...
I think I'm finally learning how they must look at me.

Yea...I think I have it right down to a science.
AMERICAN STEREOTYPING DONE AT ITS FINEST.
GOOD OL' AMERICA.

House Nigger

"They couldn't have whipped me. HELL NAW!...I would've killed all them CRACKERS!" The age old language used when the negro of the 21st century speaks on being enslaved. The major consensus, especially among young Black men, is that we would have been defiant against the persecution and horrific measures of slavery. I was always fascinated by the idea of being this immaculate-profound-brave leader as a Nat Turner if I was born in the days of slavery. Would I have the gumption? Malcolm X describes the difference between the "house Negro" and the "field Negro" at Michigan State University, East Lansing, Michigan, 23 January 1963 here below,

> "...You have two types of Negro...during slavery you had two Negroes. You had the house Negro and the field Negro...So whenever that house Negro identified himself, he always identified himself in the same sense that his master identified himself. When his master said, "We have good food," the house Negro would say, "Yes, we have plenty of good food." ."What's the matter boss, we sick?" His master's pain was his pain...But then you had another Negro out in the field...When the master got sick, they prayed that he'd die. ....So now you have a twentieth-century-type of house Negro. A twentieth-century Uncle Tom. He's just as much an Uncle Tom today as Uncle Tom was 100 and 200 years ago."

So would I have truly been able to put my life and the lives of my family at risk? From the sense of being "liked" by your master, higher quality food than the slave scraps, and instead of rags, you wore your master's tattered hand me downs. Then also you may have had the luxury of laying your head down at night within the confines of your dear master. On the other hand, the opposite: torn rags, pig scraps, hay beds, and the fear of being quick to be whipped or quick to be sold. Times are immensely different now but no matter what you think, the fields are now the corporate offices and the racism there is much more subtle. The glass ceiling is even wiped so clean that you would run right into it.

We are a such a spoiled and comfortable people with our pillow topped mattresses, self-righteousness, and low carb-keto diets. It makes me wonder the path that truly would have chosen. I grew up with my good grades, then on to college, and now I sit in unsatisfactory yet anodyne cubicle within my corporate career, safe, and right under the white man. Yes, yes, I get paid for my labor with nice health benefits as well and no one has put a whip to this back but now I have a lot to lose but less than my life. I choose to not stir any pots or raise much commotion unless provoked and I smile more than I desire so they won't mistake me for the angry Black man. I call myself conscious, know my rights and history, and speak up on most injustices when I'm outside of the walls of my occupation. This type of talk seems like a house nigga whispering out in the field but still yet, a HOUSE NIGGER.

Crab Meat

GOT DAMN, CRABS GET OUTTA MY WAY...

They hate their regular ASS jobs...
With their regular ASS money and regular ASS clothes;
Niggas say they pimpin', can't keep their regular ASS hoes.
Got regular ASS kids and a regular ASS wife;
Keepin' YOU down cause of their regular ASS life...

A bucket with no lid and we still ain't free!
Trophy-win after photo finish but a punitive victory.
No cure in sight, piled in plight;
Short sighted in height...conspiracy riiiiight?
All competitive, crawling stagnate
To diminish the valiant, is it support or challenge?
We choose the latter, cold and callous;
You see the balance?
Criticism cause you go against the grain,
Life looking like a paleo plate...
No white bread but pigeon-fed for my race...
I'm supposed to cut off my leg and then go race?
NAAHH! That's just not how I was fuckin' raised!
As I took a trip to Egypt and left my sheep behind;
Journey for alchemist legend began within the rubble of mine.
Oh LORD! I've been crawling from them...TO DESIRE!
On the journey to demise but ....somewhat Pryor...
A match went a blaze and my brain caught fire!

Momma say, "*Baby, just wait for a sign*".
Sister say, "*Girl, you ain't even that fine*".
Uncle say, "*Man, you'll never get signed*".
Daddy say, "*Boy, don't waiste your time*".
The Hood say, "*Shit, that shoulda' been mine*"...

The hate and discontent; you can understand in retrospect.
Black folks got a lot of problems, we ain't let go of yet.
Pinchin', snapping, all relentless; fuck forgiveness, fuck your feelings;
We make friendships based on delicious vengeance.
Pay market price to white folks....
And WANT THE HOOK UP FROM BLACK BUSINESS.
Fuck repentance, we've been sentenced...
To idle slaughter since forefathers;
Lid open, but by what fish monger?
White hands watch this portion, gory but dormant;
Protagonist of social status.

THEY HATE US CAUSE THEY AIN'T US!
The worst of it, we're of our own catalyst.
Dozens to halt one ensures the collective demise.
ESCAPE the bucket!...ESCAPE the bucket!...ESCAPE the bucket!

FUCK IT!..JUST KEEP EATING ONE ANOTHER ALIVE!

Just Like You
(Happy Father's Day)

I'm not mad...BUT FUCK YOU!...
I will never forget that when I turned 13,
When I thought I had turned into a man, I asked my mother...
For my father's number; and with a huge chest of gratification,
I gave him a call...he seemed excited to hear my voice,
After I told him who exactly I was.
Then I waited to hear..."*HAPPY BIRTHDAY, SON!*"...
I waited until I realized he didn't know what "today" was;
Because of that I can't make myself call him on Father's Day.
Neither on any of his birthdays but I remember every year, 6th of April.
I couldn't bring myself to go visit after his near death surgeries either.
And I picked up the phone but couldn't dial after his mother passed...
12 years later and still a slave to this animosity...and honestly...
Wherever you are...I wanted to look just like you, walk the way you do,
Be big and strong just like you...
Have the complexion of night with the smile of morning just like you.
Often into arguments with my momma...
She say I think too much like you.

I even wanted to talk just like you...
But for years you haven't said a word so now I'm forgetting...
Who you are, you conceived the sun after you made love to a star;
Then left your footprints and vanished like the sole (soul) of the moon.
And then forever went away...
Do you even remember January is my birthday?
Did you ever know any of my teacher's names?
How I still cry over my grandma?
And how I have your shoulders and arthritis?..
And how our eyes are the same?
I look in the mirror and can see how I'm stained,
I try to get you off my mind BUT CAN'T GET YOU OFF MY FACE!

As a child, only in my head because I was afraid to ask out loud...
"Why I gotta deal with this pain and Mommy...
How he a stranger and we look just the same?"
He never said a thing...but I dreamt of a father that said something like...

"Dear Son, I'm sorry I was not there nor did I teach you to...
But keep your elbows close, protect your chin, and lead with the jab.
Balance through the soles of your feet on the pedals,
I should have been running right next to you, holding the handle.
Make sure you soak the stubble with hot water...
Long slow strokes to avoid irritation.
The fat end lower than the skinny, over then loop under;
Tighten the knot till you see a natural dimple form.
Look a person in the eye, stand tall...chin up...
Cause being black is beautiful and painful but know you're a king.
Listen more and speak less...but when you speak...speak with confidence.
Success will be nothing without integrity...forever keep yours.
And when I look at your face...I see a better me;
You are my son but you are not my mistakes.
Walk like a god and your goddess will come to you,
Care for others...always protect your mother...I believe in you..
But always believe in yourself...and read...
Read every book in the library because the pages are the pallets...
That hide the keys to the chains on our minds.
And if you didn't know from my actions....I LOVE YOU, SON."

But you never said a thing...I don't know you at all and somehow...
I still love you...wherever you are...Happy Father's Day.
Sincerely,
The Product of Your Absence

Inspired by Jay-Z "Where Have You Been" (2000)

Caine's Theory

YA'LL WAY OUT IN THE FIELD!...way, way, way out in the field!....
The FIRST MURDER was committed by one brother to another.
Yo, and I'm the ambassador of this notion...
The bastard of the flamethrower that mastered the hand held explosion.
I evolved and revolved until rapid fire for the Civil War.
Liberals wanted to kill me but Conservatives funded my world tour.
Only if the cost of a single "Me" was more than the firearm;
Point blank range, I claimed all of your Civil Rights leads,
Malcolm at the Audubon, Martin on the balcony,
Evers in his own driveway but those were pale predecessors...
To my much "darker" demand.
Oh my most cherished inventions...THE GLORIOUS GANGS!
The 70s were nice but the 80s and 90s...
MAN! I really did my MUTHAFUCKIN' THANG!
Been shooting through black flesh ever since...
AM I MY BROTHER'S KEEPER...am I my brother's keeper?
Well yes, yes I am...doing exactly what I want you to do.

I'm called the devil but the true antagonist is YOU.
But I can't lie I don't mind that I'm to blame;
For the killings of lives well under age.
Well, who the fuck told you to label me with their names?
I'm not the white man, you should know I don't discriminate.
Niggaaaa, COME ON, SON, you really don't want no peace.
When you give me all I need to succeed.

Black Lives Matter but to who?...
The stance is just downright silly, fool.
Have you seen the numbers that your own have slain?
Your brotha stepped on your shoe or beat you in a $50 dice game...
I was there when you put your best friend on a t-shirt;
And I'll be there when your mother rents you a hearse.
I went from expensive military use to easy access in inner city schools.
In Jimmy's rifle and Jamal's Glock 9...
One is an outcast and one is down to ride.
AM I MY BROTHER'S KEEPER?...well yes, yes it is I.

One upon...twice upon...thrice upon a time there was a boy who died;
Meets the passion pastime of hunting down his own kind.
"Caine, teach em' how we grew up was bullshit."
But he got a hard dick for pulling drive-bys.
Kids shot donw on the playground but no "snitch" to be found...
And he just loved to hear that BLAOW!..BLAOW!...BLAOW!
Ended up taking his own mother's first child.
The connect wanted a deal, his brother wanted out;
Same momma, different daddy, fought to make their momma proud.
Jealousy of the oldest, lead to a fatal shot in his momma's house...
"I feel sorry for your mother."
Senseless crimes, exploding hearts just by inches;
Fortified henchmen, born innocent made out of brown children.
"I'M JUST AROUND THE CORNER", said Vengeance....
What is it about killing that makes you niggas feel so alive?
The sword you lived by, so the sword will be your demise.
"Caine, DO YOU CARE WHETHER YOU LIVE OR DIE?"

Caine's Theory.

Inspired by film "Menace II Society" (Hughes Brothers, 1993)

Chronomentrophobia

LIVING IS A BITCH! Then you exist till one day by death you're found.
Forever is just a collection of nows, never done verbs,
And some too forgotten nouns and...
Time ain't finna fly its way down from the sky.
Seeing the bigger picture is hard while blind...
And appreciating precious moments is even harder when outta time.
 CHRONOMENTROPHOBIA, the fear of clocks...
The fear of time...tick, tock, tick, tock, tick.

GOD DON'T MAKE NO MISTAKES!...
But I swear he running late!
My present presence isn't as pleasant as I planned;
With what my Lord had scanned, a barcode to play the system.
Now, now, no I'm not playing the victim…
I'm just describing my symptoms.
The pallet of the blood was coated for me yet the pocket watch, tick
That Benjamin carried to predict solar eclipses, tock,
Seems not too sufficient on CPT time, tick...
We "cater-pillaring draculas" with jail and death.
So coon, cocoon comfy in a cozy box.
Where the hour glass is my master and I am a slave, Young Toby,
Let me tap dance for Massa...Massa, let me mask my anger
And smear this black shoe polish all over my face.
And Bojangle in Morris Code all over this stage,
The greatest minstrel show on earth forever replayed.

Haunted by the past, frightened of the future...
I heard that as soon as you're born, you begin dying.
So more than anything else I've been terrified of "timing".
I hit the "sleep" button over and over to deny what's on the other side,
Grew accustomed to this fear;
Multiplied 100 times over throughout the years.
Compulsive clock checking...
So how many accolades before I die can I get cause as early as age 10,
I was in fear that I wouldn't be shit.
I'm talkin' fear, fear that the man in mirror becoming something...
And losing himself in the process, I'm talkin' fear.
Fear of family death because they love their pork
But won't take their meds.
I'm talkin' fear, fear that I will fail my wife and kids;
Cause I don't know nothing what a good father or a good husband is.
I'm talkin' fear, fear that I will die randomly by some nigga
That I don't even know at 7-Eleven by estranged bullets...
Buying my baby girls some gummi bears.
And the news will simply factor my life and death to gang relations.
I'm talkin' fear; fear that time simply is not on my side.
Because it has shown to be the antagonist of so many I knew and know.
So I'm down right scared with every bit of me, down to my soul.
Tick, tock, tick, tock, tick, tock....tick.

I hear clocks whispering, "Nigga, if no one else, you gon' fear me."
This predictive system is predators chasing us,
For the quickest killing, chasing us,
Illegitimate villains chasing us, legal lynchings chasing us,
Be very afraid... mind what I tell you...
Young nigga sag yo pants, young nigga do yo dance,
Young nigga smoke that trance, young nigga watch them hands.
The hands of time. CHRONOMENTROPHOBIA!

CAUSE I FEEL LIKE I AINT GOT MUCH TIME LEFT, MY GOD!
Warm that meal up in the presence of mine enemies.
Please let my testing and not my ignorance read as my eulogy..
SO THIS IS NOW MY CONFESSION!..
You are now reading my suicide letter,
Horrified of destiny and what I was becoming...
It was a must that I MURDERED THE OLD ME!
To evolve into the MAN THAT I'M SUPPOSED TO BE!

CHRONOMENTROPHOBIA.

Inspired by Outkast "Chronometrophobia" (2006) & Kendrick Lamar "FEAR" (2017)

Talkin' White

As my cousin slices his Swisher Sweet in half, sprinkles some "good" into it, and rolls it up; he then licks the creases to secure the contents. He then looks down at my tailored olive chino pants and tasseled loafers with no socks and said, "Nigga, don't ever come over my house wearing them skinny "white boy pants" again!"

See this exchange is an amusing example but nothing new with a lot of my friends and family. Matter of fact, I've always been told that..."Niggas don't do that, Niggas don't talk like that...Niggas don't dress like that...Niggas don't go to college...and Nigga, if you want to do anything out of the norm then you're "actin' white". I just decided I didn't want to be that Nigga! So hello, allow me to re-introduce myself...My name is Cordney Dewayne McClain. I was raised in a single parent home, with a hardworking mother whom kept two jobs. Among a gang violent environment topped with drug dealers and addicts and the result is: I dig raw sushi, zip lining, Radiohead, and Imagine Dragons, all while reading The Mis-education of the Negro, wearing fitted suites, and the occasional bowtie and suspenders...Yea, and Beethoven's Symphony No. 9 is dope as hell but I could listen to No. 3 all day. Honor Roll, good credit, corporate job, and a master's degree are a few anomalies that I find in my back pocket; along with the lint from Sallie Mae (Oh, the ails of scared ambition). I was actually damn good at fencing but played basketball because that's what the homies were doing.

My Big Momma once told me, "Boy, you can't sleep "white" and talk "black"! The ability to just "BE". To never bleach this Negro painted all over my face and running through my blood in this downpour of white American hegemony. To hold on tight to the negro and not be labeled would be some magnificent type of peace. The history of the American Negro is the history of this strife – this longing to attain self-conscious manhood. To merge his double self into a better and truer self.

I make sure to enunciate my words and try not to say "ain't, "yall, and "finna" within the confines of my corporate job. And while I'm with the homies and family, I place my colloquial euphemism and Ebonics right back in like a subconscious mask that I parlayed. Within this emergence, I never wanted either of these selves to be lost, the Negro or the American. So, as I wear my suspenders, listen to Beethoven and Too Short, eat my lunch at my corporate job decorated finely with not fried but grilled chicken accompanied with sweet potatoes and sautéed greens with a cup of watermelon on the side...all while "TALKIN' WHITE", please do not misunderstand who you are dealing with. This is an immensely "BLACK MAN"...in EVERY BEAUTIFUL SENSE of the term.

God Complex

TAKE HIS HEAD OFF!..
Cause if you wait for the downfall of the king,
GOD WILL NOT MAKE IT SOUND.
The devouring of the tops of pyramids by the clouds;
DARKNESS SWALLOWED THE NILE...
LIGHTNING RIPPED THE SKY!
Isis SCREAMING with a thousand of knives.
Fierce winds WHIPPED her mile long black locks;
Echoed through the tombs SHAKING my forefathers.
Numbing coldness GRIPPING Egypt's heart.
I, son of god Osiris, baptized in the stars, swaddled in the night.
The same darkness found my father murdered by treachery...
His own brother Seth, slaughtered my people then sold my flesh.
I WAS PUT HERE TO AVENGE HIS DEATH.

"Stolen from my world and brought to a new.
My masters changed and so did my words.
These strange languages they made us speak.
A new world I was a prisoner of and as a child I forgot myself
My country, my family, my identity
Everything I never knew about me."...

Emasculated me, taught me how to hate me;
Took my father away, disguised my greatness in their history.
Put dope and liquor in my hands.
Around my neck, an empty studded chain,
Shackled my feet with name brands.
Threw a hoody on me so I can't BE RECOGNIZED.
Over my face, some dark shades so I can't SEE THE LIES.
Equipped with a subpar education to not ACTUALIZE SELF;
Complete with a gun in my sagging pants so I CAN KILL MYSELF.

"As a boy, I became lost in this foreign land.
With no sense of identity, reached out to be like my oppressors.
Viewing my reflection as a curse, religion as the reinforcement.
I was raised to be irrelevant in a country for liberty
Symbiotic that all of my heroes were white
That I matured within a deep complex inferiority."...

But lately...I been feeling, I been feeling...
I BEEN FEELING LIKE A GOD!
So WHAT UP GOD! So WHAT UP GOD!
We are royalty in amnesia, tortured mind with no anesthesia.
Convicted villain and given a pale Jesus;
But we are kings without treason to make the earth fall to its knees.
I breathe and the axis moves a few degrees.
We are royalty with a loss of memory but with an inner instinct.
A buried prestige ah! WHAT UP, GOD!

"They shot the noses of the sphinx and cremated them into scrolls
We scribed our greatness but they crumbled them up.
Infiltrated the accomplishment and set the truth to a blaze.
But the temples are still the temples,
Because they house the god within you."...

If we all are made in God's image then HIS FACE IS MINE.
Wait or is that BLASPHEMY? No, it's logical it has to be.
If mine is not of my FATHER's then my conception is BASTARDLY;
Matter of fact, HE LETS ME CALL HIM ME.
WHAT UP, GOD! Treachery's head, I'm severing with a blazing axe;
Against those that oppose our dreams and goals.
I will paint their family trees with THEIR OWN BLOOD.

Their entrails will mark the sight of their deceit...
Then set the world on fire to claim our royalty.
I'll strike down with a hammer like Ogun.
WHAT UP, GOD! Master of my fate, captain of my soul.
My troops stampede with an ordained force;
We were trapped by the brain and let out by the Main Source.
WHAT UP, GOD! I'm more ruthless; move over Lucifer.
I am the water, fire and universe which means...
I'm flooding like jewelers, burning jugulars, and crushing Jupiter.
With great VENGEANCE and FURY,
Fueled anger for those who poisoned and destroyed.
MAN PLANS WHILE GOD LAUGHS...
So I snicker at the miniscule misery Time has.
I was brought here a slave flawed,
This world stamped me with a prisoner facade....

BUT I WILL, I WILL, I WILL...LEAVE HERE A GOD!

ABOUT THE AUTHOR

Cordney McClain has obtained certifications in areas such as Financial Literacy Education, Project Management and Business Process Improvement. Passionate about educating black youth, he has taken that education and conducted financial literacy workshops throughout the Oklahoma City Metro area. He has also served as Education Chairs for corporate companies, partnered with diversity councils and assisted in establishing relationships for The University of Oklahoma Outreach and minority mentoring programs. He is a member of Kappa Alpha Psi Fraternity, Inc., a soldier in the Oklahoma Army National Guard, and co-founder of Brothers 4 Progress, Inc. A husband and the father of two toddler girls, Cordney has his Master's in Business but since the time of his adolescence has studied the art of rhyming and fell in love with rap and its poetry origin.

As an artist, Cordney's zealous yet eloquent messages pursue to inspire, evoke emotion, and present visions while giving a front row view of his personal narratives on race relations, class, religion, and personal evolution. His writing addresses the injustices as well as the beautiful complexities of this world with passion and a human sensitivity for shared experiences.

BLACKER THAN SHAKESPEARE'S INK:
THE DIARY OF A NOSTALGIC KID

88791544R00071

Made in the USA
Middletown, DE
12 September 2018